Sébastien Jean

21 Day Workshop.
July '89, Belvedere.

Strategies of Love

Mose Durst

The Edwin Mellen Press
Lewiston/Queenston

Library of Congress Cataloging-in-Publication Data

Durst, Mose, 1939-
  Strategies of love.

  Includes bibliographical references and index.
  1. Love--Religious aspects--Christianity. I. Title.
BV4639.D88   1987   241'.4   87-12389
ISBN 0-88946-209-7 (alk. paper)

The Edwin Mellen Press
P.O. Box 450
Lewiston, New York
USA 14092

The Edwin Mellen Press
P.O. Box 67
Queenston, Ontario
CANADA L0S 1L0

Printed in the United States of America

CONTENTS

Preface

Several years ago, when I was living in California, I received a telephone call from my brother in New York. In a sad voice he explained to me that my dad, who had been ill for some time, had died. I flew back to New York and met with both of my brothers and their families, as we prepared for the funeral. Since my dad did not have a close relationship with a member of the clergy, my brothers asked if I would offer the eulogy for him. I consented, although I never considered what it would mean for me to eulogize my father. I frankly had never imagined the day when my father would no longer be living.

I entered the funeral home where the eulogy was to be delivered, and I asked if there was a chapel where I could pray. I was taken to a small, quiet chapel a few feet from the room where my family had gathered. Before I began to pray I had no clear idea what I could possibly say about my father. After several minutes of prayer a thought came to my mind: What is it I most valued about my father? His love for me and others came the reply.

I finished praying and returned to the room where my father's casket lay and where my family was sitting quietly. As I looked at the casket, I began to cry, for I realized that the man who gave me life and who caressed me and spoke to me was now dead. The ceremony began and I was asked to come to the podium.

When I began to speak I realized, as the words came out of my mouth, that everytime my dad had looked at me, he looked at me with eyes of love. Every time he touched me, he touched me with hands of love. Every time he spoke to me, he spoke to me with words of love. Certainly his love was imperfect, but nevertheless it was the most enduring quality about his life that helped shape and then transform my life. It helped me understand the preciousness of life and, as I would grow as a man, it allowed me to understand the reality of God's love.

The reality of my father's death not only allowed me to understand the centrality of love to his life, but it moved me to reflect on the importance of love as the core value to all life.

A second experience that happened this last year encapsulated for me the significance of love as a transforming force, and it was the final motivating stimulus for me to write this book. My five year old daughter asked me to buy her a book about Rainbow Brite and the Color Kids. Since there is nothing that delights me more than to buy someone a book, I quickly purchased several books in what was a series of stories about Rainbow Brite.

Each story, which my daughter has asked me to

read to her dozens of times, is about Rainbow Brite, who colors the world with her star sprinkles and makes the flowers, trees and sky beautiful. She lives in Rainbow Land and must always encounter the ugly, resentful Murky Dismal and his sidekick Lurky. Murky and Lurky, who live in the Pits, are always trying to remove the beautiful colors from the world and make everything a dull gray. Fortunately, Rainbow Brite rises to each challenge, overcomes all difficulties, and is able to triumph over Murky. At the end of each story the world is renewed in its beautiful color.

As I interpret this child's story, Rainbow Brite paints the world with the colors of love. Forces there are which seek to destroy this love, but she is able to prevail over them by wisely using strategies of love to overcome all difficulties. My daughter loves Rainbow Brite, and I have been able to explain to her that my job is to be like Rainbow Brite in trying to transform all the Murky's and Lurky's of the world and in ourselves.

Whether it be the experience of death, the reflection upon what is significant in life, or the analysis of a child's delight in a story, I have come to believe that love, given and received wisely, is the ultimate creative force in life. Although transforming relationship through love is difficult, because it involves awareness of the self and sensitivity to the other, many strategies can be used to overcome the difficulties.

Introduction

As a college professor for fifteen years and as a church pastor for fifteen years, I have had occasion to observe the importance of love in the lives of many people of various ages. I have perceived a pattern that reappears in life after life as people are touched, shaped and transformed by the power of love. I have seen people magnified by love, and I have seen people diminished by love. I have marvelled at how people use wisdom in developing strategies of love to enhance life; and I have anguished at how love is not received, not enlarged, and is of no avail to life.

The thousands of people I have known lead me to believe that human beings are truth-seekers, beauty-seekers, and love-seekers. They expect from the world an experience which is truthful, beautiful and lovable. The mind sorts through, sifts out and seeks to discover that which is true. The emotions reach for and quiver to the stimulus of beauty. The heart motivates us to connect well with that which we experience: we want to love the object of our experience.

I have never met anyone who sought not to understand, or who sought to be pleased by confusion. Our emotions do not look to be stimulated by ugliness. If Picasso doesn't please us, we search out the harmonies in Piero della Francesca. But we cannot live without our sense of the beautiful. I have

4

not met anyone who sought not to love or be loved.

Many of the people I have known in my religious work have been blessed with a genuine religious conversion experience as they made their journey through life. They were stripped of all superficial sensibility and seemed to experience the depth of their being, and the core of Being itself. They experienced a profound love, became aware of transcendent ideals, and identified with the universal human community. Their "conversion" experience literally turned them from the habitual to the radical and transcendental. They moved from a concern with "mine" to a concern with "Thine."

I have been aware of seeking for ideals in my life, and I have also experienced a religious conversion that made me aware of the universal and eternal reality of God. What I have observed in myself and others, however, is the necessity to sustain the larger vision of an ideal while learning how to work with the obstacles to the realization of ideals.

It sometimes happens that after experiencing a radical conversion, we begin turning back to the habitual mundane norms of life. Our heart may close and we may feel the cold indifference of relationship. We are mentally burdened by the trivial, pained by the loss of our glasses. We become very aware of the obstacles within us that make us feel incapable of reaching out or loving the other. We may feel insecure, inadequate or unloving. We may begin to lack courage, we do not want to be hurt, we are alone.

Simultaneous to our awareness of the obstacles within, we may become frightened by the obstacles without. I have known some people who felt deceived by their transcendental conversion, for they became aware of an only too imperfect world. I have known others who felt wounded by the ice-pick sharpness of the world, and ran for shelter from their ideals to someone or something that could bring them comfort. No one escapes from life without in some way being hurt by the world.

The obstacles within and without are very real to all of us. They may dim our awareness of great love and large ideals, yet most of us I have found would choose to liberate ourselves and liberate the world if we knew how. Even if we profess a great religious conviction, we need to be redeemed, each day, as we redeem the other. We need to activate strategies of love.

We find the pattern of redemptive love exhibited in the strategies of the great religious figures: Moses, Jesus, and the contemporary saints. What we find in their lives is an example of strategies that we must all employ if we are to be healthy individuals, building loving families and communities and thus co-existing in a peaceful world. The challenge of defining, employing, and succeeding with strategies of love is not just the challenge of the religious life, it is the challenge of all life.

Chapter One

The Ideal of Love

"And thou shalt love the Lord thy God with all thine heart, and with all thy soul and with all thy might."

Deuteronomy 6:5*

To sustain our ideals, especially the ideal of love, we must first define the nature of the ideal then develop strategies by which the ideal can be nourished and sustained. If we are religious people who believe that we have a relationship with God, we must look at our nature to see how it resembles God's nature. In doing so, we identify the source of our ideals both within and without. Only in this way, by understanding the essence of our nature, can we truly nurture our ideals.

If we are created in the image of God, as the *Bible* teaches us, then we must have a nature, an "original" or essential nature, that resembles God. If

---

* All quotes are from the authorized King James version of the *Holy Bible*.

we believe that God is loving and good in His essential nature, then it should follow that we desire, above all else, to be loving and good. We can understand, too, if we look within ourselves, that our nature seeks to express itself in purpose and action. Therefore, our mind seeks that which is true so that we can be connected well with that which we know. Our emotions are stimulated by beauty so that we can feel at one with the beautiful. We seek to do the good with our will, for we ultimately love that which is good. All of our relationship with the world is rooted in our desire to be connected well with that world. We want to enter into loving relation with all we know, feel and do.

We are inspired, moved and uplifted by words and stories of love. The words "I love you" are the most powerful in any language. The stories of Antony and Cleopatra, Othello and Desdemona, Romeo and Juliet move us to the core of our being. We read True Romance and imagine the ideals of love in the lives of Prince Charles and Princess Diana. We are comforted to see Nancy Reagan look admiringly at her husband with a twinkle in her eye. We know they are in love. My happiest moments as a child came as I watched my mother and father dance in the kitchen to the waltzes of Johann Strauss. Even mom and dad could participate in the magic and mystery of love.

The great appeal of religion, I believe, is rooted in the ideal of love that religion stimulates in our original nature. When in Judaism we learn to chant, "Hear, O Israel, the Lord our God is One", we feel that a loving God is at the center of creation. When we realize we are created in His image, we know we have infinite energy, infinite creativity, to be infinitely loving. As we chant and pray to God we enter into relationship with the source of all existence and the center of love. Many Psalms of the Old Testament are love songs in the life of faith, which is a life of love. In Psalm 51 David sings,

> Have mercy upon me, O God, according to thy loving-kindness; according unto the multitude of thy tender mercies blot out my transgressions.
>
> Psalm 51:1

And in Psalm 84 David sings,

> How amiable are thy tabernacles, O Lord of hosts!
> My soul longeth, yea, even fainteth for the courts of the Lord; my heart and my flesh cry out for the living God.
>
> Psalm 84:1-2

In Psalm 116 David offers the gratitude of one redeemed:

> I love the Lord, because he hath heard my voice and my supplications.
>
> Psalm 116:1

9

In the Song of Solomon we hear a love song of Solomon that can be interpreted as a love of God for His covenant people:

> My beloved spoke, and said unto me, Rise up, my love, my fair one, and come away.
> For, lo, the winter is past, the rain is over and gone
> The flowers appear on the earth; the time of the singing of birds has come, and the voice of the turtledove is heard in our land.
> The figtree putteth forth her green figs, and the vines with the tender grapes give forth fragrance. Arise, my love, my fair one, and come away.
>
> Song of Solomon 2:10-13

Many stories in the Old Testament are testimonies to the great love of men and women toward each other and toward God. They inspire us by the depth and profundity of their love, and they awaken within us the possibility that we too are capable of such great love. The heroes and heroines of the Old Testament have always been moral examples, object lessons of faith with and in love, models for all those who need to grow in love.

Abraham may be the father of the Jewish faith, but he is also the father of their love. His willingness to sacrifice his beloved son Isaac for the sake

10

of God was not a mindless offering to a heartless God. On the contrary, Abraham so loved God, whom he believed to be the source of all life, lawfulness, and love, that he was willing to offer that which he loved most to the source of love. Abraham understood that God had given him all that he loved and held dear, and that his very ability to love his son, and to experience the love of his son, were all gifts from a loving God.

The story of Abraham humbles us, for we see how small is our own love and ability to sacrifice out of love, yet at the same time we are inspired to see what love we are capable of, for we are connected to the life of Abraham if we are part of the Judaic tradition. We learn, also, from this story not only of the love of a son for a father, Abraham for God, but of the father for the son. God will not hurt Abraham, He will not diminish his faithful and loving son. In fact, Abraham realizes a deepening of his own love through the very process of the offering, as he realizes how much his own son Isaac loves him and is willing to trust and obey him. The loving Father (God) raises up a loving child (Abraham) who becomes a loving father and raises up a loving child. The norm of existence is established, a norm of love centered on God. Man's original nature is realized in fulfilling God's original ideal of creation, an ideal of love, in family over generations.

Judaism is spoken of as the religion of Abraham, Isaac, and Jacob. The pattern of love realized between Abraham and Isaac is one that can resolve mistrust, hatred and breakdown in relationship. Jacob is the true child of his father. His story repeats the essential example of love that is at the heart of religion. If human history is characterized by brother slaying brother, then religious history, God working in human affairs, is a restoration history where unity, harmony and love triumph.

The story of Jacob and Esau is one of restoration. Jacob must show such love to his brother that hatred and discord are dissolved into love. Esau has many good reasons to hate Jacob. When has hatred not had "good reasons"? He can enumerate, catalogue and classify those reasons. He cannot go beyond his hatred. He does not desire unity, harmony and love in his relationship with Jacob. One could argue, too, that Jacob has many "good reasons" to hate Esau, to avoid him, to ignore him. Yet, Jacob is aware of his original nature, of God speaking to that original nature. "Hear, O Israel, the Lord your God is One". One God, one love, one human family. Jacob must work to reconcile himself with Esau, even if he has to suffer for many years. He knows that he has only one purpose that can fulfill his life: he must love his brother.

As with the story of Abraham, we are humbled by the greatness of Jacob's love for his brother. Who among us would endure such hardship for the sake of love? The power of love in the story also uplifts us, for we know that it is possible, not only for Jacob but for us, to go beyond ourselves in loving another.

From the same lineage of Abraham, Isaac and Jacob we find another hero of love. The pattern remains the same. In the midst of resentment, oppression and hatred from his own brothers, Joseph responds with a heart of forgiveness and love. It is not enough to ask the cause of hatred by Joseph's brothers for him; there are a myriad reasons for hatred. What is more important to ask is why Joseph does not hate. Why does he respond to hatred with love?

I suggest that Joseph allowed the call of God to touch his original nature. The call of love must have been nourished, as virtue or character is nourished: by other noble stories of his ancestors, by his own internal discipline, by the religious ethos around him. It is not enough to feel "called" by God. One must develop the calling through nurture and discipline. Joseph understood that he must restore his relationship to his brothers as one of love. He took responsibility for this restoration process because he was aware of a great ideal of love, and he committed himself to that ideal. The teaching and the example of his ancestors became real in his own life. He could have followed the example of Cain; instead, he chose to follow the example of Jacob by offering a purer love to his brother.

We could pursue the ideal of love in the lives of the noble women of the Old Testament. The sacrificial spirit of love is exemplified by Ruth when she

13

faithfully clings to her mother-in-law:

> Entreat me not to leave you or to return
> from following you; for where you go I
> will go, and where you lodge I will lodge;
> your people shall be my people, and your
> God my God; where you die I will die,
> and there will I be buried.
>
> Ruth 1:16

Hannah, the mother of Samuel, knows that her child is not her child but God's. She prays for a son, but she offers the son to the God she loves even before he is conceived:

> O Lord of hosts, if thou wilt indeed look
> on the affliction of thine handmaid, and
> remember me, and not forget thine hand-
> maid, but wilt give unto thine handmaid
> a male child, then I will give him unto
> the Lord all the days of his life.....
>
> 1 Samuel 1:11

Esther has no fear when it comes to the love of her people:

> ...so will I go in unto the King, which is
> not according to the law. And if I perish, I
> perish.
>
> Esther 4:16

This is neither a small nor narrow love, and

we name our daughters Ruth, Hannah, and Esther because we hope that they will love like the heroines of the Bible.

When we encounter Moses, we find an example of someone whose love for God and his nation is so great, and who is able to overcome so many obstacles, he becomes the supreme example of love that we find in the Old Testament. We often see Moses as the "liberator" of his people, but we just as often forget that the motive of that liberation is a great love. Although Moses grows up in a palace as the son of an Egyptian princess, he feels compassion for the suffering of the Hebrew people. He sacrifices his comfort, his safety and the love of all those who have raised him for a greater love.

Moses feels called by God to rescue a people, and his original nature responds to that calling. The response, however, must not have been simple or short. If Moses is going to be God's champion, His example of love for a chosen people, then he must develop a love that is as large, as absolute, and as unchanging as God's love. He must be able to maintain his commitment to that love through hardship, betrayal, loneliness, confusion, anger, resentment and all the other difficulties that beset the ideal of love.

What happens when Moses initially begins to help the Hebrew people in Eqypt? They become frightened that the Pharoah will oppress them with a greater harshness than they have ever known. They want a liberator, yet they don't want a liberator who will make their lives more miserable. Moses himself probably didn't realize how difficult it would be to love and to liberate his people. He is not necessarily wise in the way he seeks to liberate them for he lets his anger overcome him when he slays an Egyptian. Is this love, to slay another? Perhaps not; therefore, God has to see if Moses' love is genuinely for the sake of His providence, not for personal grandeur. Moses must go through a longer and greater course of suffering as a test of his love.

After Moses establishes his family, he is strongly called by God once again. "Moses, I need you; my people need you; go and rescue them." What is Moses to do with this new calling? He now has a wife, children, property. Once again he will risk everything if he follows this calling by God to save the Hebrew people. Moses doesn't even believe he is capable of responding to God's call: after all, he is no longer a young man, he cannot speak very well and what will the neighbors say?

"Moses, I need you. Yes, it is true, you are not very good, but you are the best I've got. So go! What have you been praying for all these years? Why have you been studying? For a Ph.D.? I need you to love my people; they are stubborn and stiff-necked, and they need someone more stubborn and more stiff-necked to love them. Go, my son, go, I will be with you."

16

So Moses decides once again to enter into the drama of liberation and love. He leads the people out of Egypt and into the desert. Is he now comforted; have the people understood how they too must follow the faithful example of God's love? No. Day after day Moses encounters hardship. The people begin backbiting: "Moses doesn't know where he is leading us. He is a religious fanatic, just like the fanatics in Egypt. In fact, he has created a cult mystery around this mumbo-jumbo, mountain-top experience with God. Why couldn't we all go to the mountain top? Why does God only work through him? God told me this morning to go back to Egypt. Let's start a go-back-to-Egypt movement. He doesn't really respect us Hebrews, he is always criticizing us. Who does he think he is anyway? I'll bet he actually hates us and is just looking for his own power. Why don't we take responsibility as mature members of this religious community: let's make a golden calf and show Moses that God is a great and mysterious God and that he loves us all, no matter what we do."

Moses must have truly agonized as he saw how the Hebrews failed to understand even the most basic things about the lesson of God's love. When they felt good, yes, they seemed to understand everything and to be very obedient to Moses' teaching and example. When they felt bad, however, humility, sacrifice and obedience stuck in their throats like so many dry bones. God needs to raise up not only Moses as an example of His love, he needs a people, a Chosen People, to be an example to the world, not merely an

17

example of intelligence, of diligence, and of endurance, but primarily an example of love. God needs a people to take responsibility for raising up the other peoples of the world to the standard of His love. Such is the purpose and function of a Chosen People.

For forty years the Hebrew people wandered in the wilderness. It was as much a spiritual wilderness as a physical wilderness. More so. A generation had to die before God could have hope that a new generation would be innocent enough to seek to do His will. Even Moses disobeyed God out of his own personal anger, and he too would never enter into the new and promised land of love.

The story of the Exodus is repeated ceremonially by Jewish people during the Passover celebration each year. It is a story that is told over and over again because it is a great love story. It is a love by God the Father for his children, and it is a love by Moses, who sought to act with God's love, on behalf of the Jewish people. We always need to hear this story, especially at times when we feel oppressed and unloved. The exodus story has been the favorite Old Testament story of black people in America, certainly during the time of slavery. They knew what it was like to be slaves, but they knew that their loving Father would empower them to accomplish a mission of liberation.

The Life of Jesus

The life of Jesus is the greatest love story ever told. It is a story of a Father who lovingly offers His son for the sake of the world, and of a Son who, for the sake of His Father and the world, offers His life and love in return. The Gospel of Matthew, which tells the story of the life of Jesus, is said to be the most influential book in the history of the world. When we read the words of Jesus we are inspired by a love that is entirely good, pure and true. Our original nature responds with a desire to imitate that example. Throughout history monks, sages, and ordinary people have sought to model their lives in imitation of Jesus.

> Ye have heard that it hath been said, Thou shalt love thy neighbor, and hate thine enemy;
> But I say unto you, Love your enemies, bless them that curse you, do good to them that hate you, and pray for them who despitefully use you, and persecute you.
> That ye may be the sons of your Father, who is in heaven; for he maketh his sun to rise on the evil and on the good, and sendeth rain on the just and on the unjust...
> Be ye, therefore, perfect, even as your Father, who is in heaven, is perfect.
> Matthew 5:43-45, 48

We often gloss over, interpret away, or ignore this last sentence that Jesus speaks, for it is here that we are confronted with a standard of love by which we are to live our own lives. We may truly be inspired to see the quality of Jesus' love, but when He challenges us to perfect our own love, we dismiss His meaning as if He were only being poetic. But certainly the essence of the conversion experience is the "turning" away from a worldly love whose standard is measured by the reality of the world, toward a heavenly standard of love as exemplified in Jesus. If we are moved by the spirit of God, if our life changes dramatically as we dedicate ourselves to God, then the focus and quality of our love changes. The world is often confused and chagrined as it perceives something "abnormal" taking place in such an individual. Yet, the standard of normality is usually the way of the world, not the way of God.

The world was confounded by Jesus because what He was preaching was the simplest truth, the truth of love. With all sophistication and complexity, the world is often confused as it fails to recognize the innocence and purity of love.

> Master, which is the great commandment
> in the law?
> Jesus said unto him, Thou shalt love the
> Lord, thy God, with all thy heart, and
> with all thy soul, and with all thy mind.
> This is the first and great commandment.

> And the second is like it, Thou shalt love
> thy neighbor as thyself.
> On these two commandments hang all
> the law and the prophets.
>
> Matthew 23:36-40

These words of Jesus are perhaps the ones most often preached and perhaps the ones most given lip service, although they are the ones most difficult to live, and therefore most violated.

Jesus, however, not only preaches the words, He lives the words. He teaches, heals, serves, suffers and even dies for others. His entire motivation and action is to live for the sake of others. When He is persecuted, He responds with love to those who persecute him. He has every "good" reason to return the world's indifference and hatred with withdrawal and resentment. Nevertheless, He continues to transform those around Him with the power of love, rather than to annihilate them with the power of hatred. He clearly understood that the essence of love is unselfish and sacrificial action on behalf of others.

Perhaps the supreme example of Jesus' love comes at the moment when He has the most reason to despair, to give up all hope and love. He has trusted in His Father in Heaven that love will prevail; He has offered his love to the world, and yet He appears to have been completely rejected. As Jesus seeks to give life to the world through God's love, the world responds to Him with a murderous hatred. He is nailed to a cross, mocked, and reviled:

> And they spat upon him, and took the
> reed, and smote him on the head.
> And after they had mocked him, they
> took the robe off from him, and put his
> own raiment on him, and led him away
> to crucify him.
>
> Matthew 27:30-31

As man abandoned God at the beginning of
history, it is perhaps fitting that God should seem to
abandon Jesus at this critical point. Jesus has the opportunity of abandoning God and even the love of
man at the moment of death. Instead, what is His response:

> Father, forgive them; for they know not
> what they do.
>
> Luke 23:34

At the time of His death, Jesus seemed to the
world to be a total failure. Two thousand years after
His death, Jesus' love has triumphed over the failures of the world. The love offered by Jesus is the supreme value, absolute and unchanging, it remains
constant. The world offers many values that are rela-
tive and changing, but they pale in comparison to a
love that is true. A central function of the Christ, the
Chosen One, is to teach the world how to love.
What is it the world needs most? True love. What
is it that God most wants to teach the world? True

Love. What is it that will be most difficult for the world to embody? True Love.

If the world did not trust, believe and follow Jesus' example of love, they at least have continued to be inspired by His words and spirit of love. The disciples could be faithful or faithless, but they could not deny the value of a God-centered love. Even those who never knew Jesus directly could be moved to preach His gospels. The history of Christianity is filled with the lives of saints, martyrs, and sacrificial men and women who sought to imitate the life of Christ.

Paul was a rabbi who cruelly persecuted the early Christians, whom he believed to be heretics. When he experienced the spirit of Jesus on the road to Damascus, he underwent a dramatic conversion, and dedicated himself to a life of love, rather than a life of persecution. Perhaps the words most quoted from the Bible, ones that expand our definition, are those of Paul on love:

> Love suffereth long, and is kind; love envieth not; love vaunteth not itself, is not puffed up,
> Doth not behave itself unseemly, seeketh not its own, is not easily provoked, thinketh no evil,
> Rejoiceth not in iniquity, but rejoiceth in the truth;
> Beareth all things, believeth all things,

hopeth all things, and excuseth all things.
1 Corinthians 13:4-7

Paul lived, suffered and died for the sake of love. He followed his words by example when he urged the members of the small Christian community to imitate Christ by making themselves sacrificial offerings to God.

Who were some of the saints inspired by Jesus and Paul? They were sanctified persons who determined to set their lives apart to God inviolably for His possession and service. Through suffering, trials and torture they were unwavering in their love for God and humanity. St. Peter Martyr, a Dominican preacher, killed on his way to Milan, wrote "Credo In Deum" in his own blood as he died. Saint Julitta, a Spanish noblewoman, was sawn in half for her refusal to deny her Christian beliefs. Saint Lawrence was asked by the Romans to hand over to them the treasure of the church. Instead, he handed them the paupers of the church. For his insolence, he was burned to death.

Some people try to explain away the radical behavior of the saints by saying that they were definitely not normal people—perhaps they were under some form of mind control or neurosis, for they seemed possessed by this love of God. Yet for them this was the supreme normality of life, the greatest good and the highest ideal they could live for. All of us (who have had conversion experiences) have moments when we feel like we can offer our lives for the sake of God or those we love, but those moments are short-lived. The difference between the saints and us is that although they too might have struggled with their ideals, their lives are testimonies to a triumphant love.

The ideal of love is at the heart of a true religion, for a God of love is at the heart of the universe. Since we are created in the image of God, our original nature will always respond, to some degree, to this ideal of love. The challenge, however, is to make substantial this ideal as we overcome the resistance within ourselves and the obstacles presented by the world.

The ideals that have inspired readers of the Bible for thousands of years are the source for modern religious movements of renewal and revival. If God is a living and loving God, then He is as alive today as He was 4,000 or 2,000 years ago. He will work in similar loving ways to guide His children. The world always finds great mystery in God's ways, and indeed love is the greatest "mystery", yet what is mysterious to us is very clear and normal from God's point of view. God is love and will seek to fulfill his original ideal of love, the ideal of creating a peaceful and loving world, in each generation.

If we role-play God for a moment and look at the world, what are the greatest obstacles to God's ideal of love? What are God's greatest headaches?

War, racism, selfishness exhibited in various forms of decadence and immorality, and God-denying ideologies like communism that stress violence and the destruction of human life. Religious bigotry and other forms of hatred can be enumerated. Certainly God has other agonies, but I have listed some of the most tragic and destructive.

Who, then, will God look for as an object of His love in this age? Anyone, presumably, who seeks to embody His heart, His ideal, His purpose and His will. God works through many people to fulfill His will. The same was true at the time of Moses and Jesus. God's need in this age is for someone to continue the process of restoration until His Kingdom is established on earth as it is in Heaven. What is central to God's Kingdom? The ideal of love.

The religious leaders in this age will teach the same ideals of true, sacrificial love that we read of in the Bible, although we might suspect that they will receive the same hostile reception as the saints who came before them. We may still be inspired by the words of love, but the sacrificial reality of love is a fundamental challenge to our lives. Especially if one says he comes with the spirit or mission of Christ, we might be warned that such a one will be mistreated. Usually we fear that we will be abused by an anti-Christ, but actually we act like anti-Christs in abusing our Christ figures throughout history. I don't feel confused about anti-Christ figures: they speak and act with hatred, malice and murder. They are the

Hitlers, Stalins and Maos of the world. It is the Christ figures who challenge us with the Biblical ideal of love whom we resist.

The Reverend Sun Myung Moon

I am a follower of the Rev. Sun Myung Moon, the founder of the Unification Church. He has been a man despised, vilified, imprisoned and tortured in several countries. Nevertheless, he has created a worldwide religious movement, in more than 120 countries, including dozens of cultural, humanitarian, and business projects. What is it that this man teaches, and why has he been able to inspire so many followers? He follows in the same tradition as the teachers of love in the *Bible*.

When he was sixteen years old, like many other teenage children, he wondered as to what purpose he should dedicate his life. Through prayer and meditation he experienced a vision of Jesus Christ and he felt a calling to fulfill the mission of Christ. By this he understood that he must discipline himself to love the world as Christ loved the world, and then to seek to bring loving unity between families, nations, races and cultures. This was a beginning point.

For the ensuing nine years he focused on continued prayer, study and acts of service and charity. He was confirmed in his calling. In the 1940's, while he was a student at Waseda University in Japan, he helped organize a resistance movement against the Japanese oppression of the Korean people. For this action he was imprisoned. Later, in 1948, he went from South Korea to communist North Korea to preach the Christian Gospel. He was arrested, imprisoned in Hung-nam concentration camp for almost three years, then liberated by the U.N. forces in 1950. He traveled to South Korea and eventually established the Unification Church in Seoul in 1954.

Although this is a broad sketch about how the Unification Church was founded, we might look more deeply at the internal motivation of this religious teacher and see if he has anything in common with the historical heroes of God's love. First, central to Rev. Moon's teaching, in the original Korean Church and in the worldwide Unification Church today, is the belief that God suffers because of how His children abuse, misuse, and violate the ideal of love. In teaching about the suffering of God, Rev. Moon seeks to inspire and exhort humanity to liberate God from His suffering by correcting the abuse of love in human affairs.

The Unification Church in Korea has been called the "Church of Tears" for all the tears that have been shed for God's suffering. Rev. Moon's sermons and life are examples of purity, humility and devotion. He has prayed more, cried more, fasted more, and worked harder than anyone the members of the church have ever seen. He lived in the back of the Church with his family until he moved to the United States in 1972. Although there was sufficient wealth for Rev. Moon to live in a luxurious home, for the Church had grown to a worldwide movement by 1972, he continued to live in the church building until coming to this country.

Rev. Moon came to the United States because he believed God called him to bring spiritual revival to this nation. America, Rev. Moon believes, is a central nation in God's providence, and it has a special mission to be an example of God's ideal to the world. Unfortunately, however, Americans have been destroying their nation through personal immorality, family breakdown, and a lack of understanding as to how to serve the larger world. Rev. Moon has inspired thousands of Americans to dedicate themselves sacrificially for the sake of God and the world.

The reaction to Rev. Moon could have been predicted by historical precedent. Instead of being praised for inspiring others to high ideals, he has been accused of exploiting others through base motives. He has traveled throughout America, sometimes giving fifty sermons in fifty states in fifty days, but has been accused of sitting home in idle and luxurious indolence. He has created numerous charitable, humanitarian and educational projects, from a graduate seminary to various relief foundations, but has been vilified as the magician-svengali who could be seen in the dark side of the moon, creating monuments to his own magnificence.

What kinds of words does this Korean man speak to inspire so many? The universal words and language of God's love:

If we know the air is full of radio waves we cannot see, then we can understand how in God's world the air is filled completely with the electricity of love. Once a circuit is complete, electricity can do many things. If today's electronic communication is just a shadow of what God's world is like, then we know that nothing is impossible in God's love. Then it is also clear that a spirit world must exist.

If we experience God's love for a time while we still have a physical body, then in spirit world we will continue in the same intensity of experience. The spirit world is full of the electricity of love. You know that at the flip of a switch all the buildings in New York could be lighted instantly. Heaven comes on earth when all the lights are lit to their brightest, and heaven in spirit world is where all the lights are love, and they are fully lit.

If your subject of love moves, you don't have to reason or think—you automatically move with it. The air of spirit world is love, and so in spirit world you cannot help wanting to love everyone, wanting to have banquets to invite everyone to. Such a thing can happen instantly, at just the thought of it. What do you eat in spirit world? The food of love. In love, the more you look, the more you want to look. The more you listen, the more you want to listen. You would never tire of it. Dullness and tiredness have no place there. How could you be tired when there is so much excitement? If you are full of happiness, could you sleep if you were told to?

You would want to give much love to others, and thus to present yourself in a beautiful way, so you would want to have big jewels. God has everything. It's not that we need to own these things; when we complete the circuit of love, God gives us what He has. Some people say I am a dreamer, but if I have logic and reason to back up what I say, I am actually a realist. If there is a possibility that I am right, then this is worth trying. With this expectation, we will try and see what happens. There is no question that you are already hooked by my thought![1]

We have seen now how a religious ideal of love involves dedication, sacrifice, unselfishness, endurance, courage and determination in seeking to do God's will or in serving others. Love is not merely a desire for an object that pleases or benefits us. Even if God is not at the center of our love, an ideal of love would encompass great service to humanity or to a people. The biblical tradition of love is a standard by which we can evaluate the religious teachers today, such as Reverend Moon, and it is a measure of our own love. Although many of us might agree with the parts of this definition, we would also have to acknowledge the difficulty in realizing such an ideal.

FOOTNOTES

[1] Reverend Sun Myung Moon, "Life of Experience in the Realm of Heart" (New York: HSA Publications, March 15, 1981), p. 4.

Chapter Two

Challenges to Love

The Obstacles Within

Although we are inspired by the ideals and examples of love, and some of us are moved to imitate the lives of those great figures who sought to live lives dedicated to love, we quickly find that love may be the ideal most sought after but most rarely found. We find challenges to the realization of love both within and without.

Central to love is the offering of one self for the benefit, welfare and happiness of the other. To offer oneself, to sacrifice oneself, for the benefit of others, however, is not easy. The way of the world is such that we think first of our desire, our happiness, our benefit and how the other will fulfill our purpose. It is as if all of human history has etched out a slippery slope, now deeply grooved, where the "rational" direction of individual desire moves downward toward oneself.

If changing this direction, so that we think of

God's purpose or the well-being of the human community as our first priority, were easy, then the tragedy of human history could have been corrected thousands of years ago. What is this tragedy? The hatred of one individual by another, by one family of another, nations warring with other nations. Human beings have indeed acted like odious vermin rather than creatures created in the image of God. We have defiled the earth, despoiled human culture, and profaned God as we have focused on selfish lust, greed, and license. Even our saints have been suspect, and George Orwell writes that saints should be assumed guilty (sinners) unless proven innocent.

All of us at times find that between our ideals and our actions falls the shadow that paralyzes us. We have read that it is better to give than to receive, but we find it easier and often more pleasant to receive. We have heard that it is more virtuous to act for the benefit of others than ourselves, yet it seems so foolish for us to do so and suffer the opprobrium of the world. The spirit is often willing, yet the flesh is more often weak. Sloth, Gluttony, Lust, Pride and their friends are not now so commonly named as our companions, yet they are our real friends whom we spend much time with each day. We seek the land of ideal love, which is high on a hill, but we end up in the slough of despair.

Whether our culture produces more of a "me generation" than others can be debated. However, we have enormous opportunities in this culture to avoid authorities that would focus us on ideals, norms, standards or values that transcend the self. The self can very easily be the measure of all things and the center around which all things must revolve. We don't want to be burdened with weighty moral decisions in reference to standards of value, so we choose that which is "Lite".

A recent article in *The New York Times*, entitled "In the 'Lite' Decade, Less Has Become More", illustrates how thin our moral sensibility has become.

> Light is a way of thinking that we've come to in the 80's, says Dr. Robert T. London, a psychiatrist at New York University Medical Center. It's an umbrella phenomenon where lightness transforms itself into the cars we drive, the lightness in a room, our diet, as well as lightness in the relationships we have.

> Sociologists say that 'lite', which started as a marketing term used to denote dietetic products, has become a metaphor for what Americans are seeking in disparate parts of their lives. In their relationships, for example, they have turned away from soul-searching and stress of emotional commitment....[1]

We turn away from the stress of relationships because of the pain of relating. If we are to relate, if we are to love, then we must give a part of ourselves to the other. But if we do not feel our self grounded in anything larger, then we fear that we do not have very much to give, and we must calculate that anything we give must be given under the condition that we receive something back—quickly.

We can fall in love, with another person or with God, and feel temporarily enlarged by merging ourselves with the other. But unless we develop the habit of offering a genuine part of ourselves to the other, we soon have "a falling out", and we once again feel the insecurity and weakness of being thrown back upon our small selves. Perhaps the greatest obstacle to love is that we look within and feel we do not have very much to give. We feel small, insecure, inadequate, fragile, weak, alone and empty. We can pump ourselves up with the allure and outer trappings of love, but we are, in T.S. Eliot's phrase, "the hollow men."

From the scintillating secular cafes on the West Side of Manhattan, where young, fashionable and attractive professionals gather in crowds, to the sedate middle class, properly-dressed congregations at Southern California revival meetings, we form groups in search of a power to propel us in our relationships. As human beings we need to be connected to something greater than ourselves, yet we grope for relationship without knowing how to build, through time, the purposeful solidity of relationship. After many frustrations we begin to lose our ideals, our love and our hope. We just want to get by.

We fail to realize, as we encounter the frustrations of loving, that love is not necessarily a momentary emotional high that takes away the feeling of emptiness. Love, rather, is the disciplined process of mind, emotion and will in which we create consistency, stability and strength in relationship focused on purpose. Like a great work of art, a human life of beauty is built over time through consistent, purposeful, virtuous action. We need not be too frightened by our feelings of inadequacy because in many ways we are inadequate before we become adequate. Immaturity must be the stage which precedes maturity. Our chief concern should be the direction of our growth.

Before we are mature in love, we are immature, so we need to develop love through discipline and purpose over a lifetime. The major point is that we have a purpose or an ideal for our love. If we want to imitate Christ in our lives, then that is a noble purpose to guide us. We should not be discouraged however, if in pursuit of our purpose we exhibit behavior which is immature, un-Christlike.

A young member of my church came to see me recently and explained how discouraged he was in his life of faith. He regularly felt unable to love other people and was highly critical of their shortcomings. For years he was motivated to serve people or to embrace them, but he would often feel unable to overcome his strong sense of judging himself and judging others. He believed in a loving God, but he could not understand why God did not help him overcome his frustrations.

Now this young man was only in his mid-thirties, and had only decided to dedicate his life to an ideal of God-centered love at the age of twenty-five. For the first twenty-five years of his life, he had been a person living without much clarity or purpose beyond his own personal interests. Through a religious conversion experience he began to focus his life on activities that could be of benefit to the larger human community. He had developed many virtuous qualities in serving others, yet he had many qualities he still had to work on. Rather than seeing all of his life as a process dedicated to his ideals, he focused on one particular point in the process, within himself, that was discouraging, and so found it difficult to maintain hope.

At any one point in our lives we can look at ourselves and see weaknesses that have been with us from our earliest moments. The child is father of the man, said William Wordsworth, yet the child within ourselves often frightens us as a throwback to our immature, atavistic self. If we focus on this particular part of ourselves and forget the overall process and development of our lives, then we are thrown into the limits of our vision. We no longer have the hope and power to create something noble of our lives; we are pinned against the wall by a pointed image of our weaknesses.

We are all sinners, and we are all weak. However, we are more than sin and weakness. I have often grieved over the action of an immature pastor who, to motivate his congregation, will dwell on their shortcomings as he seeks to spur them to action through guilt and fear. This technique may work in the short run, but it will certainly fail in the end. Since we are all imperfect people, we can be made to feel bad and guilty about our imperfections. The danger of dwelling upon shortcomings, though, is that we may not yet have developed the vision or the strength of character to direct us toward a positive image of what we might become. The devil has always been with us; we have just heard about the Christ.

Inevitably in a life of faith, or a life dedicated to an ideal of love, we will confront within ourselves all the weaknesses to which the body and the spirit are heir to. Hamlet might look on the one hand as noble and loving as a god, but he is insecure, confused, impulsive, cruel, neurotic, and vengeful. His life is a failure because he dwells on his impulsive and cruel qualities rather than on learning to control and overcome those impulses in service to some larger ideal.

We all have more than a little Hamlet within us. We may not go around murdering everyone who has injured us (although this seems to be happening more frequently), yet within our spirit we harbor a murderous resentment or a cruel and cold indifference. When we act in such a way we know it, either consciously or unconsciously. We cannot fool our "original" nature that seeks to reflect a God-like ideal of love. We begin to suspect that our life is a failure, a contradiction, an absurdity. We become aware of the gap between what we might be and what we are. Finally, we believe, like Hamlet, that we cannot act to fulfill our ideals or we act rashly to violate these ideals. Thus we have the tragedy of Hamlet as well as the tragedy of all human life. We have a potential to reflect our divine nature fully in love, yet we violate that nature and make of ourselves a base and cruel stuff.

In one sense we can define Hamlet's tragedy, and also the human tragedy, as a failure to employ strategies of love. Hamlet is trapped by his limitation, a failure of love being a failure also of the imagination. He is urged on by the ghost of his dead father to avenge a murder. He sees this action, then, as his central purpose, and the possibility of redeeming his step-father through love is not ever entertained. Hamlet never discusses his situation with anyone. He never works with anyone to help him resolve his conflicts. He doesn't imagine the full range of possibilities of clarifying his purpose.

The great stories of literature and of the *Bible* illustrate for us the dilemmas that face us as human beings. Perhaps the most revealing story is that of

Adam and Eve in the book of Genesis. Whether one takes the story literally or symbolically, it is certainly an archetype of the failure of love, of failing to employ strategies of love. God blesses Adam and Eve as he tells them to be fruitful, multiply and have dominion over the earth. Rather than fulfilling the blessings, however, Adam and Eve violate God's commandments. Eve is tempted to follow an authority and a love other than God's. What is Adam's situation?

Adam is obviously hurt by how Eve violated God's trust and commandment. He is aware of how he loves Eve, yet he must have been confused when she tempted him as she was tempted. What can Adam do? He means well, so perhaps he should just try to comfort Eve by going along with her desire and also ignoring God's commandment. Adam does not go back to God and ask what he should do. He can always ignore God's advice, but he does not even ask to hear about any possibilities or strategies God might offer him. Would it not have been possible for God to offer Adam a strategy for redeeming Eve rather than joining her in sin?

I recently visited a church member who I had heard was confused and depressed. As I entered his home, I was led to a dark living room, drapes drawn, with objects lying randomly about the room. In our conversation I learned that the man was out of work and no longer had much hope for his life. He no longer understood God, he did not believe prayer worked for him, he did not trust leaders in the church, and his only pleasures were playing sports with friends. I asked if he would like to share with me so that I might help him. He was skeptical that I could do anything for him. I asked if he trusted anyone who could be of help to him. He told me of another friend with whom he shared his feelings. Unfortunately, his friend was also somewhat depressed as he had become cynical about life and about "organized" religion. Both friends decided to abandon their life of faith and go to Alaska to find their fortunes.

This example was very painful because these two individuals exhibited no desire to understand the obstacles to the fulfillment of love in their lives. Further, they did not attempt to figure out strategies by which they could overcome those obstacles. Everyone at some time feels terribly hurt and closed to the love of others. We shut ourselves off, "turn off" much of what might help us, for we believe we are justified against what has hurt us.

The feelings of hurt, pain, betrayal, abuse, and violation are the most universal justifications people offer for not loving others. We all have been hurt many times and we usually remember those hurts vividly and precisely. We categorize them like stamps in a commemorative stamp album. "Here is what he did to me five years ago; there is the pain I suffered from in 1982; there is an agony from 1985 I will never forget—or forgive." We not only remember our pains, but we will not forgive the one who has hurt us, and we thus feel totally justified in not extending to the one who hurt us.

Sometimes I imagine that the world is like a beautiful, colored balloon filled with a poisonous dark gas of anger and resentment. Everyone seems to carry around hurt, anger and resentment and no one seems to know how to dispose of it. It is a kind of waste product, like nuclear radioactivity, which has the potential of destroying everything, yet we do not know what to do with it except let it out with Chernobyl-like explosions that frighten or kill a few people at a time.

The stored up anger, pain and resentment within us I perceive to be the greatest obstacles to the ideal of love. We suspect, or already know from experience, that the act of loving another will almost certainly bring us more pain. We don't like pain. Unless we are mature enough and disciplined enough to transform pain into love, compassion or beauty, unless we are poets of the soul, we know that more pain will diminish us.

Mother Teresa was interviewed on television some years ago and was asked by the television host how she felt working with lepers in India. She replied, "It hurt, at first." The host was surprised at her response. "How can you, a saint-like person, talk about pain in dealing with these people? I thought you loved them?" "I do love them", she replied, "that's why it hurts me to see them suffer. However, when I see that I can be of some comfort to them, then I feel joy."

Most of us stop when we feel the pain of relationship; we don't see ourselves as transforming, redeeming agents of love. We would much rather judge those who are hurting us, place them at a distance, where we see them critically, rather than lovingly transforming them.

If we develop, through patience, discipline, and hard work, a parent's heart in relationship to our children, then we do not take their cruelty as a blow to our self. We do not, if we are mature parents, fix our children with a judgment that leaves them pinned and wriggling on the wall. Rather, we seek to love them, to educate them, to show them by our example what they might be.

When Jesus tells us to judge not, lest we be judged, implicit in His remarks is that we must instead transform with love. The easiest thing in the world is to hold off another at a distance, emotionally or physically, and judge him or her. The most difficult thing is to let someone close enough so he or she might hurt us, then to be strong enough to respond with love. Since our souls cry out to love, for the sake of our own authenticity we must love, or else we lose our souls. In truth, there is no way to avoid pain in relationship, for if we withdraw and pretend that we have no relationship to the other, we wake up in the middle of the night, screaming, and we wonder why we are having a nightmare.

The story of Cain and Abel in the *Bible* is of course the archetype of the relationship where someone feels hurt, cannot overcome the feeling of hurt with love, and so destroys the one who causes the pain. Cain probably had many good reasons for his resentment and many explanations as to why Abel was unworthy of his love, deserved to be hated, needed to be killed. "Why did God accept his offering and not mine?" Cain must have thought, "What an unjust God. I spent more time and did a better job on my offering. I loved God more. Abel never really loved God. Also, after God accepted Abel's offering, Abel was so conceited, arrogant, proud. He wasn't kind to me". And so like Adam, Cain fails to think about how God would view this situation. He sees only his own situation, feels only his own pain, and acts from his own point of view. Who has committed murder, in spirit or body, and not felt justified? What nation has gone to war against another nation and not felt justified? And how many in history have been the redemptive agents of God's love?

"He hurt me, I'm angry, I won't have anything to do with him, I don't need him, I'll strike back." This is the usual sequence in human affairs. If we ignore the sequence in Biblical literature, we can see it in the everyday, common-place taxi ride in New York City. A taxidriver feels cut off by another taxi; he ignores it for a while, just a few foul words coming out of his mouth; he blows his horn, watches carefully in the side mirror, then he cuts quickly to the right narrowly cutting off the first taxi. Several horns blow at once. "I'll get him at the next intersection" is the thought now in the heads of both drivers.

Closing ourselves, remaining closed, or striking out at the one who we believe has hurt us has consequences. First, we fail to grow our spirit of love. If we are bound up in relation to the other, a failure to enlarge the other is a failure to enlarge oneself. Second, both the self and the other are diminished by any failure to reach out actively and enhance the other. Let me illustrate this mathematics of love.

Some time ago I invited two friends of mine whom I had not seen for some time to dinner. They both happened to be visiting New York City, where I lived, so I asked them for dinner to a restaurant I thought they would enjoy. After an initial greeting at the restaurant both of my friends began speaking to each other about their experiences over the last year, they told several jokes that only they would understand, they carried on parts of conversation in a language I could not understand and, to my amazement and incredulity, parted from me after dessert with a terse farewell.

During the entire course of the dinner my emotions ranged from anger, resentment and hostility to a feeling of being struck with arrows like St. Sebastian. Of course my thoughts were un-Sebastian-like, for I was not thinking of my Lord as I was being pierced with arrows of indifference. I was caught by surprise in the most unusual dinner meeting I had ever experienced. I wanted to leap across the table and grab my friends by their throats, for I was verbally unsuccessful in shifting the direction of their conversation. To add insult to injury, they seemed completely unaware of my discomfort.

My wife met me shortly after my friends had parted and when she asked how I enjoyed the dinner, I let forth a torrent of expletives. She was more than a little shocked. She began to point out the obvious lesson that even if my friends may have acted like brutes, I should have still embraced them with a loving spirit rather than a more brutish hostility. I had let them define me (literally "to define" is "to limit") rather than my changing their definition (their "limits") with a transforming attitude.

Further, as I let forth angry words after the dinner I actually undercut any moral or spiritual ground upon which I could be redemptive. By undercutting my own moral position, I had lost, they had lost, and the spirit of evil had triumphed. I could speak words of love, but I had removed the ground of moral authority that could be the example of the love symbolized by the words.

As I evaluated my behavior I realized that I had not disciplined myself enough in overcoming the obstacles within my heart, mind and soul. I let my feelings of hurt and insecurity block my desire to love and embrace. I focused on my situation from my point of view rather than their situation from God's point of view. Because I did not like getting hurt, I got hurt. Because I did not think of love, I could not love.

Spiritually, like a guide leading me by the hand, my wife was able to help me clarify the pattern by which I dealt with the obstacles to love. I could see clearly that unless there is a guide to reveal the pattern, there is no way to develop strategies of love to overcome the obstacles.

Finally, in terms of describing the obstacles within that block us from realizing the ideal of love, we must realize that there are some obstacles that cannot be clearly explained or analyzed. Edgar Allan Poe wrote a short story called "The Imp of the Perverse" which describes a perverse power within human beings that make them feel and act in unpredictable ways. Nathaniel Hawthorne in numerous writings, such as his short story "Young Goodman Brown", writes of a power of darkness within people that makes them do destructive things for no apparent "reason". We must be prepared to admit that there is a kind of darkness or destructiveness within us that can neither be completely explained or completely removed.

As a religious person I could explain this perverse nature as that which we human beings have inherited from our fallen ancestors who rebelled against God. But even if I explain that an evil force, Satan, works upon my fallen nature to make me act in destructive ways, I have not explained away the obstacles within. At best I am placed on guard to know that I must try to control the propensity for evil. I am warned to avoid environments and situations that can enlarge and set loose this force. Thus, St. Paul warns us that we should pray twenty-four hours a day. He understands that if our mind and heart, our internal being, is not focused on God, then another force has the potential of destroying our being.

The Obstacles Without

As we turn from the obstacles within that block us from the fulfillment of the ideal of love, to the obstacles without, we are confronted with a mirror image of ourselves. Like a husband who is angered by his spouse because her weaknesses remind him of his own, we are angry that the world is no better than we are. It is probably fair to say that by looking in the mirror we have a pretty good idea about the state of the world. The world frightens us at least as much as we frighten ourselves.

The obstacles presented by the world are real, they are not merely figments of our imagination nor are they projections of our neurotic paranoia. If we look within ourselves and find fear, anger and re-

STRATEGIES OF LOVE

sentment, we can also look up and find that the world is very much a fearful, angry and resentful place. If we look within and feel hurt, we can also look out and see that we can get hurt.

A simple act like getting the evening newspaper can be a journey to the nether world, to hell and back. When I am in New York City I stay in our church headquarters building on Forty Third Street between Fifth and Sixth Avenues. At about ten o'clock in the evening the next morning's newspaper is out on the stands, and since I enjoy reading the paper at night I like to pick it up at a newstand in Times Square between ten and twelve o'clock.

It is only three blocks from the church building to the newspaper stand, but I might as well be Odysseus journeying to Hades in overcoming the dangers of the streets. First, the corner of Forty Third Street and Sixth Avenue has become the hangout for drunks, drug-pushers, and foul-mouthed, unstable street-people. If I make it past this set of obstacles, I am confronted with the dark, wine-smelling doorways of the next street. Twice, while walking down the street, I witnessed a criminal running wildly down the street with a gun in his hands, frantically being chased by several policemen with drawn guns. Finally, if I make it to Broadway, I am confronted with the lewd marquee of pornographic movie theatres and the lascivious reality of street hookers.

Now, granted, mine is an unusual neighborhood, not exactly Sesame Street, it is becoming less and less unusual in the United States to be a victim of crime, drugs, and sexual violence of one sort or another. If we don't feel safe going out for an evening stroll, how do we feel about our children walking about the streets? Last week I gave a speech to a group of ministers on the problem of drugs. My airplane landed at Newark Airport at 10 am, and I was to speak at a luncheon meeting in Manhattan at 12 pm. Driving into Manhattan I witnessed two drug sale transactions within 45 minutes.

Policemen are now stationed in front of the public library in New York because drug pushers were becoming so numerous and so aggressive to passersby. When I was a child growing up in New York, the stone lions in front of the library were enough to deter some criminals, now we need troops. Last week I wanted to take my family to a movie in New York City; I checked the listing of some fifty different films but found not one without a theme of sex and violence. Finally, in desperation, I looked under the section in the newspaper for film revivals and found several Charlie Chaplin films being shown on 95th Street and Broadway.

To attract movie patrons, advertisers genuinely seek to seduce us by stirring our sexual passion, our anger and our destructive impulses. Very few films seek to enoble us by appealing to our Christ-like potential or by showing us heroic lives of purity, chastity and service to humanity. Yesterday's *New York*

Times [2] presents the following copy on the film pages:

> *Reform School Girls*: "So young...So Bad...So What?.... Shocking!!"

> *HardTraveling*: "The Times were Hard...Decent Men Were Driven to Desperate Acts."

> *Bullies*: "Heroes aren't born...They're cornered."

> *Night of the Creeps:* (No comments were offered next to this title, for the lurid imagination of viewers could suffice.)

Since we all need and want love, ideally a true, genuine and real love, we must open ourselves, make ourselves vulnerable, to other human beings and to the environment in order to receive this love. The cruel shock of life, however, is that people and places violate us rather than nourish us. Even those who genuinely want to love us often hurt us. When we first discover that our parents do things which hurt us, we are shocked. Usually, we recover from this shock by realizing that the overwhelming number of things our parents do for us are done out of love and for our benefit, not to diminish us. If our family is basically healthy, then we develop compassion, forgiveness and understanding for those who hurt us, especially our parents. The family well-being is enhanced as each member is committed to healing hurts.

If the family is not a healthy unit, then it is difficult to overcome the hurt, pain and other obstacles to the realization of love. If a child is abused, he learns to fear—not to love. If he overcomes his fear, he does so often to express anger rather than love. If a child is treated with indifference, he feels distant from the world, which he perceives to be a cold and indifferent place. Many of our attitudes about people and situations that we cling to as adults we had thrust upon us as children. The pain and abuse inflicted upon us as children, therefore, are very real obstacles to the fulfillment of love.

If as adults we are confronted with people who are selfish, unloving and imperfect, we have learned to build up defenses against being hurt too badly. If we know that people will hurt us, we keep our distance from them so that they cannot hurt us too badly. We may smile and smile, but in our hearts we are knaves and will not let on that we do not trust the other. Friendships are not often ones where, like those recommended by Aristotle, we seek to draw out the ideal of the good from the other. Rather, we cultivate friends rather like we cultivate tomatoes in our garden—for our pleasure, our use and our taste.

I am always more than a little astounded as I meet public figures at receptions and participate in conversation. Upon being introduced, rarely is a name spoken so that it can be understood. Of course there is no acknowledgment as one speaks one's own name. I have been often tempted to say, "Hello, Dickens is my name, Charles Dickens; ah, yes, you have a lovely bleak house." It is not practical in large gatherings for one to have deep encounters with everyone, but surely there can be more sincerity in individual conversations. After a conversation is struck up, one invariably mentions "My good friend so-and-so", or "My dear friend...." My experience has taught me that these dear friends are often "contacts" that are practically useful, but often with little genuine friendship involved.

As up we grow, then, our ideals come tumbling down. We learn from our own experience and we learn from older people that the world is a cold, cruel place. We are confronted with people and environments that are selfish, unloving and imperfect. Consequently, we lose our hope of making the world a place that resembles our ideals.

By failing to take responsibility for transforming our environment or relationships, we imagine ourselves as victims of circumstance. As victims we become more and more passive, action becomes impossible; we become critics of all things and lovers of none. If we act out our ideals at all, we do so in fantasy, in art or in some small way that brings us the pleasure of cultivating our own garden. We become less public-minded and more driven to the pursuit of private pleasures.

We are all aware of obstacles within and without that prevent us from realizing our ideals. We try our best to overcome those obstacles, but usually our attempts are intuitive, impulsive and unsystematic. If we can identify clear strategies of dealing with these obstacles, we can begin to liberate ourselves from frustration and a sense of guilt. Further, we can begin to become transforming agents of our environment, actors in the human drama rather than victims being acted upon.

FOOTNOTES

[1] Robert T. London, "In the `Lite' Decade, Less Has Become More," *The New York Times* (August 13, 1986), pp. A1, A16.

[2] August 24, 1986.

Chapter Three

Strategies for Overcoming the Obstacles Within

Prayer

The cornerstone of the religious life is prayer. It is the central means by which we establish relationship with God, and it is thus the primary way in which we overcome the obstacles to love within. If God is the source of life and the source of love, then it is incumbent upon us to relate to Him continuously if our life is to be vital. The fall of man away from God, and also the result of any sin, separates man from God and makes man feel as if he is trapped within himself.

"God is not dead, he just doesn't want to get involved," reads the graffiti. It is not God who is dead or uninvolved, rather it is ourselves until we learn to pray. Prayer gets us involved by opening our relationship with God, by making us aware of our closeness to each other as children of that same God, and by giving us an awareness of our divine nature which is connected to all things. Prayer allows us in the most sincere way to extend the deepest part of ourselves to the Divine other. As we become aware of our relationship with God we realize we are not alone, we are not powerless and we are in contact with a great source of energy, meaning and love.

As prayer opens us up to the greatness of God, it simultaneously makes us aware of our relationship to greatness. "The world is charged with the grandeur of God, it shines out like shook foil," writes the poet Gerard Manley Hopkins. The poet, like the one who prays, becomes aware of the mystery and majesty of all creation, especially of oneself. Not only does prayer awaken us to an experience with God, but we become aware that there is an intimacy and personal bond between ourselves and our Creator. We begin to discover that we are created in the image of God, that we have a parent who seeks relationship with us, His children.

If when we feel overwhelmed by the obstacles within, we focus on ourselves and are therefore unable to reach out to others, prayer allows us to shift our focus outside of ourselves. We begin to think about God and His relationship to the world. We start thinking and feeling from a point of view that resembles a parent rather than that of a child. "Prayer is the fundamental relationship of man to

STRATEGIES OF LOVE

God, a state of attention to God, involving the whole personality."[1]

Just as prayer allows us to overcome obstacles within as we establish a relationship with God, so too prayer makes us aware of our responsibility toward other human beings. In fact, we often need to be instructed how to pray by a teacher, a rabbi or a priest, for prayer is not only a spontaneous utterance by the self, it is also a means by which one gives organization to the spiritual life. Jesus, for example, was acting as a good rabbi when He instructed His disciples in formulaic prayer: "After this manner, therefore, pray ye...." (Matthew 6:9).

The Lord's prayer reveals to us numerous ways to overcome the obstacles within. First, we are taught to say "Our Father." These words make us aware that prayer is social, a communication with God that makes us feel our social solidarity. If we pray in unison, moreover, we can be aware of relatedness to our brothers and sisters, all of whom are children of "our Father." God, too, is a Father, not just a vague spirit or an impersonal creator. We can establish an intimate personal relationship with God as we discover the unlimited potential of our own divine nature. We can experience the great warmth and security of a true parent-child relationship.

The words "Who art in Heaven" indicate the state of being where God's love, spirit and will prevail. Heaven does not have to be remote from us, for Jesus also says (Luke 17: 20-37) that heaven is within, "in the midst of you." Further on in the prayer Jesus prays, "Thy Kingdom come, thy will be done on earth, as it is in Heaven." Jesus had preached that the Kingdom was at hand and the Beatitudes described the rewards of the Kingdom. The earth can become a mirror of Heaven if God's will is done here; heaven on earth is the place where God's love prevails as His will is done.

When we pray "Give us this day our daily bread," we petition God for the simple sustenance of our life. We thus acknowledge our dependence upon God and so solidify our relationship to Him. If we have violated this relationship, especially by feeling the obstacles within that cut us off from God, then there is a need for sincere repentance: "and forgive us our debts, as we forgive our debtors." We are thus opened by unburdening ourselves and making ourselves vulnerable to God. We take responsibility in acknowledging our failures to relate and we then feel empowered to renew relationship.

Finally, Jesus teaches us to pray, "For thine is the Kingdom, and the power, and the glory, forever." God is everything of value and we will remain cut off, empty, unless we can establish relationship with God—in which case we can then become everything. We can establish God's Kingdom of love, we can feel his power, if we connect to Him. Prayer thus enables us to break out of ourselves and realize the power of love. Even God can then be moved by the power of our prayer.

In a sermon entitled "The Importance of Prayer", Reverend Moon speaks about how :

> In churches today people pray for their denominations, their social security check or their family problems and their pet. God's ears hurt when He hears those prayers and He will plug His ears. If those people prayed for God to use their church to help save the world and liberate God, He would perk up and be amazed because God is a person just like you. When you talk about yourself in prayer, God is thoroughly bored and nothing will happen. But if you pray for His righteousness and His Kingdom, He will be caught up in your passion....The prayer for all seasons is the prayer for God's Kingdom and His righteousness.[2]

Reverend Moon's emphasis is that prayer should mobilize us toward action. Certainly we should discover God through prayer and develop a profound understanding of our own preciousness in relationship to a loving God. But this is stage one of prayer life. We may be comforted by God and receive a great solace knowing that God is our loving parent. A deeper quality of prayer life, Reverend Moon teaches, reveals to us that God suffers and we must act to liberate God from His suffering.

If God's original ideal of creation was to receive joy through the love of human beings created in His image, then God must grieve seeing how human beings abuse, misuse and violate the purity of love. Rather than making the world sacred with a holy love, we profane the world with a cheap and tawdry love. Rather than creating a loving human community called the Kingdom of Heaven on earth, human beings have acted like villains in creating a world of war, hatred and hell.

Prayer reveals to us the true situation of God and the true human situation. We can no longer be complacent, then, after a true prayer, for as we become aware of God's ancient grief and the tragedy of human history, we are motivated to act. We seek to comfort God by embodying his ideal of love in our personal lives, our families, our communities, and in the world. We get out of ourselves, move beyond our own limitations, the obstacles within, as we learn to take responsibility for comforting the heart of God and healing the hurt of the world.

Prayer then leads us to an understanding of the Biblical commandments to love God with all of our heart, soul and mind and to love our neighbor as we love ourselves. These commandments are inherent in the original purpose of God's creation. Through prayer we reflect on God's nature, purpose and will and we come to understand something about our own nature, purpose and will. We are created in the image of God, so we have love that is as infinite as

61

God's love. Our purpose in life is to love the world as God loves the world. We have a purpose like our Parent's purpose. Further, we must use our will to activate our heart and our purpose. So, too, God has been working throughout history to establish his Kingdom of love on earth.

As prayer can lift us up to feel great value and purpose, it can also humble us as we see our real defects from God's point of view. If through prayer we begin to realize our great potential for love, we also become aware of how mean and small our love has been. The infinite purpose of our life unfolds to us in prayer, while at the same time the petty reality of our lives becomes clear. If we learn to be grateful to God for the many blessings He bestows upon us, we also learn to be repentful for how we misuse those blessings.

In my own prayers I always offer gratitude to God for life, for love and for the wonderful and beautiful creation. Immediately after, however, I repent for my sins, the sins of my family, the sins of my nation and the sins of the world. I know that we have all violated God's gifts of life, love and creation. I pray for purity, innocence, simplicity and humility so that I might love the world as God loves the world and care for it as he cares for it. I pray for God's love, His wisdom, and His strength. I pray that I may do His will and comfort His heart.

When Reverend Moon was a young man of

sixteen years old he discovered in prayer that God suffered, that He worked through saints, sages and prophets throughout history to teach humanity about His ideal of love, and that Jesus' mission was to fulfill that ideal on earth. He prayed further and felt called by Jesus to carry on the mission of establishing God's Kingdom of love on earth. Throughout his life Reverend Moon has prayed to understand more deeply God's original purpose of creation, the nature of human sin, and the means by which human beings can fulfill their purpose.

Given the state of the world, anyone who takes seriously the radical call by God in prayer is seen as somewhat strange. The term "snapping" has been used by a habdfull of psychologists, sociologists and the media to describe a person who undergoes a conversion experience, who turns away from the small concerns of the self to the large purposes demanded by God. All genuine religious experience is eviscerated as the secular pundits seek to understand prayer in mechanical, chemical, and reductionist terms. As long as one prays in one's closet, the world will ignore the silence. As soon as prayer motivates one to transform the world, the world kicks back. Abraham, Moses and Jesus must have experienced God in prayer, but they were not called to the comfortable life, nor were they greatly appreciated in their lifetime by those around them. The Lord's Prayer, if taken seriously, is a most radical call for the transformation of oneself and the world. We must go beyond the obstacles within in hearing the cry without.

Study

Just as prayer awakens the heart and spirit to a relationship with God, the act of study stimulates the mind, the intellect, which also arouses the heart and spirit. For the scholar or the serious person bent on the quest for knowledge, to mention study as a means to know, to feel and to act is a truth so simplistic as not to be worthy of mention. When, however, we encounter obstacles within us which block us from actualizing the ideals of love, we often forget about the resources that knowledge can offer us in overcoming those obstacles.

All great religious traditions offer us in their sacred literature wisdom that guides us in our quest for knowledge as we seek fulfillment in the life of faith. We are not alone, nor are we the first to encounter obstacles as we seek to realize our ideals. The *Bible*, for example, may not only be viewed as the inspired word of God, which indeed can motivate us to overcome difficulties, it is also a several thousand year old record of people called to realize high ideals of love, and who either succeed or fail. By studying the *Bible* we see examples of how people like ourselves deal with the difficulties of the life dedicated to ideals.

The Old Testament, with its colorful stories of families, clans, a nation called to fulfill God's commandments, and the continual struggle to respond faithfully to God's call, is a series of moral examples that parallel our own stories and struggles. The story of our loves, our triumphs and our tragedies is the human story. It is told in every generation, for it is what human life is about.

When we read the historical narratives in the Pentateuch, we learn how God deals with his people. They are called by Him to fulfill a covenant, to obey His laws. We see how God is merciful and loving when His children obey Him, and we see how they are punished when they violate his laws. We read the prophets Amos, Hosea and Isaiah and we learn how the Israel people are sunk in vice; the prophets speak boldly about the need for virtue. In the book of Amos, God reveals his anger at the corruption of the people:

> I hate, I despise your feast days, and I will not take delight in your solemn assemblies.
> Though ye offer me burnt offerings and your meal offerings, I will not accept them; neither will I regard the peace offerings of your fat beasts.
> Take away from me the noise of the songs; for I will not hear the melody of thine harps.
> But let justice run down like waters and righteousness like a mighty stream.
>
> Amos 5:21-24

God does not tolerate any excuses for why people fail to live righteous lives. There is in the Bible no psychologizing away of the failure to live up to God's ideals. If you feel obstacles within to the realization of a righteous life, God urges greater faith and harder work. If one overcomes, then one can feel God's mercy and love.

> And in that day thou shalt say, O Lord, I will praise thee; though thou wast angry with me, thine anger is turned away, and thou comfortst me.
> Behold, God is my salvation; I will trust, and not be afraid; for the Lord, even the Lord, is my strength and my song; he also is become my salvation.
>
> Isaiah 12:1-3

Study of the prophetic books teaches us about the continuous struggle between virtue and vice, the forces of darkness and the forces of light. As we see our own lives and our struggles we can gain insight about ourselves by seeing how others have dealt with similar difficulties. When we are acutely aware of the obstacles within us, our frailties, we often lose historical perspective. We feel alone and we forget that we are not the only ones to encounter difficulties in pursuit of high ideals. Especially in the United States, we tend to be a people who are generally focused on the present and the future. It is easy for us to ignore the wisdom of the past as we frantically pursue the now and the new.

The significance of personal responsibility for overcoming one's vices and shortcomings is emphasized in the *Old Testament*. God wants His people to change their lives if they have been wicked. He does not accept ignorance or the shifting of blame for sin on others or the environment.

> But if the wicked will turn from all his sins that he hath committed, and keep all my statutes, and do that which is lawful and right, he shall surely live; he shall not die.
>
> Ezekel 18:21-23

When we turn to the psalms, songs of the spiritual life, we discover almost every facet of a life in search of God and His love. There are songs of joy and songs of sorrow, songs of anger and songs of exultation, songs of isolation and songs of union with God. Virtually every stage of spiritual life is reflected in these psalms. As we ourselves experience these various moods and stages, we can be both comforted and reassured to know that difficulties are not rare as one seeks to realize a relationship with God.

The psalms are above all acts of devotion in which God is praised, honored and glorified. Many times as I myself have felt spiritually dry, unable to identify a source of power or love within me, I have regained my connection to God and to my heart-love by singing holy songs. I have often repeated the Twenty-Third Psalm as a source of comfort at times of sadness, and invariably I have been comforted. I often sing verses of praise of God when I am joyful; I sing the lines about the great God, our Father, our King, in the Hebrew form that I learned as a child.

The stories of Job, Ruth, Jonah and the other figures found in the Old Testament reveal to us in great detail the dynamic of virtue and vice. From pride, arrogance and hatred to faith, humility and love, we watch the elevation and triumph of Biblical heroes and heroines. What is new under the sun? Nothing, when it comes to the qualities of the human character. When we feel trapped within ourselves, when we feel like sinners who will never overcome our weaknesses, it is instructive for us to read how our Biblical likenesses were able to overcome their shortcomings.

The short stories in the *Bible* function like all literature. The work of art, the story, allows us to enter into a little world and to be transformed as we experience that world. We are somewhat humbled in our sorrow when we read of Job's suffering and how he came to realize not to question the God who created him. We learn the meaning of genuine faith and sacrifice as we experience Ruth's life. Jonah offers us the awareness of small-minded goodness in contrast to God's big-hearted love. We are never the same if we genuinely enter the world of Biblical narrative.

The "wisdom literature" in our age, so to speak, is to be found in the columns of Ann Landers and the books of Dr. Ruth. No wonder that people are skeptical that study of sacred texts is of value as a guide to overcome personal problems! We make a major mistake, however, if we ignore the Bible as the wisdom literature of a people who seek God and the fulfillment of the highest ideals. Such literature offers a genuine guide by which we can direct our lives.

The Book of Wisdom in the Old Testament sets forth the fundamental pattern by which we must seek God and reject evil.

> Trust in the Lord with all thine heart, and
> lean not unto thine own understanding.
> In all thy ways acknowledge him, and he
> shall direct thy paths.
> Be not wise in thine own eyes; fear the
> Lord, and depart from evil.
>
> Proverbs 3:5-7

When we feel lost within ourselves, it is more than a little helpful to have the wisdom of a people that sought to know God and to fulfill the highest good. We continually probe to find out what is wrong with ourselves and our age; rarely do we look to what we should do to make ourselves wise and well. We need to understand wisdom if we are to be good and loving people.

By studying *The New Testament* we find a universal pattern by which we can learn to live well.

69

STRATEGIES OF LOVE

The life of Jesus is at the very least a guide for our own lives, for in his words and deeds we become aware of the greatest goodness and the greatest love. The story of the birth, death and resurrection of Jesus is truly the greatest story ever told. For thousands of years lives have been transformed by studying and imitating this great life.

Jesus' teaching is about the Kingdom and its laws. The historical Jesus comes in the context of a Jewish community that is looking for a Messiah, an anointed one, a righteous human being who will usher in God's Kingdom on earth. Jesus comes to proclaim the Kingdom. He wants his disciples to believe him, to trust him, to follow him. He never preaches that they must betray him. On the contrary, he teaches them to pray and exhort God to establish his Kingdom on earth as it is in heaven.

What can we learn of this Kingdom? By what principles is it to be governed? Jesus teaches us about the internal, moral dimension of law, while leaving the external form of economics, politics and government to the responsibility of the secular powers:

> Blessed are the poor in spirit; for theirs is the Kingdom of Heaven.
> Blessed are they that mourn; for they shall be comforted.
> Blessed are the meek; for they shall inherit the earth.
> Blessed are they who do hunger and

thirst after righteousness; for they shall be filled.
Blessed are the merciful; for they shall obtain mercy.
Blessed are the pure in heart; for they shall see God.
Blessed are the peacemakers; for they shall be called the sons of God.
Blessed are they who are persecuted for righteousness' sake; for theirs is the Kingdom of Heaven.

Matthew 5:3-10

The Kingdom, then, is a world like that around us, with people like you and me as its inhabitants. The central difference between that world and the one in which we live in is the quality of heart, ethics and love. Jesus comes to teach people to change their lives as a basis for changing the world. He is under no illusions about the difficulty of people changing their lives from self-centeredness to God-centeredness:

Enter in at the narrow gate; for wide is the gate, and broad is the way, that leadeth to destruction, and many there be who go in that way;
Because narrow is the gate, and hard is the way, which leadeth unto life, and few there be that find it.

Matthew 7:13-14

STRATEGIES OF LOVE

If we complain that we feel inadequate to follow Jesus, that there are too many obstacles within that prevent us from changing our lives, the exhortation is still clear: "Anyone who does not take his cross and follow in my footsteps is not worthy of me." Jesus does not promise us a rose garden. On the contrary, He knows that we will suffer as we seek to overcome obstacles and thus to transform our lives. Unfortunately, if we seek a great good, there is no way to avoid these difficulties.

Although Jesus' life is a testimony to the greatest love, God's love, He receives from the world rejection, scorn, hatred and death. He freely offers His life for the world, and He passionately desires that people should follow His example and live for the sake of God's Kingdom. Certainly Jesus' life is one where He affirms God's love in spite of all difficulties, within or without. By understanding the principles Jesus sets forth, and the example of his own life, we have a clear guide by which we can use our own lives for the greatest purpose.

The world may cynically reply that it is impossible to become Christlike, for we will only receive the same treatment that Christ got. This is perhaps the central excuse people give for not changing themselves. Jesus warns us that if we seek to protect our lives at the expense of the Kingdom, then we will surely die—spiritually. For those who offer their lives, suffer and die for righteousness sake will indeed live eternally. The quality of our spiritual life on earth, what we bind together here, will determine the quality of our life in the eternal, spiritual realm.

Many times I have heard from members of my church that it is difficult to become like Christ. What they often forget is that we find in the *Bible* the principles we must live by if we are to live well. If we fail to live by these principles we literally lose our souls. We may not like the choice confronting us. It may be a very serious choice. Nevertheless, we choose our own destiny by the moral choices we make. There are always serious consequences to our moral choices.

Our age often fails to provide a moral framework for our actions. Young people, especially, casually enter and abandon sexual relations without evaluating the moral consequences of their actions. Teenagers have children out of wedlock, drugs numb them, money buys them, and parents ignore them. In surveys of university students, career success and wealth rank numbers one and two in their life purposes. Books on how to get ahead sell far better than books on how to overcome selfishness and build a better world. The last thing we think of when we are in a motel room is to open the night-table drawer and read the *Bible*.

The words of the *Bible* instruct us on how to deal with the passions and pressures we feel within that confuse us. Just as Paul in his letters sought to guide the young communities of the Christian world in living a life dedicated to a Christ-like love, we can learn from his words wisdom to help us overcome our own difficulties. Paul is not ignorant of the conflicts within us, and human beings have not changed so much that they cannot learn about themselves from reading Paul.

A central theme in Paul's letters is perhaps the theme most ignored by the modern age: the reality of sin. How many of us cry out:

> For that which I do I understand not; for what I would, that do I not; but what I hate, that do I.
> If, then, I do that which I would not, I consent unto the law that it is good.
> Now, then, it is no more I that do it, but sin that dwelleth in me.
> For I know that in me (that is, in my flesh) dwelleth no good thing; for to will is present with me, but how to perform that which is good I find not.
>
> Romans 7:15-18

We should not be surprised then when we realize that we have obstacles within us that prevent us from realizing a great good. Nor should we be content to recognize that we are sinners and do nothing about transforming ourselves. Paul urges us to recognize the seriousness of sin and he exhorts us to a life of the spirit so that we can overcome sin:

> Therefore, brethren, we are debtors, not to
> the flesh, to live after the flesh.
> For if ye live after the flesh, ye shall die;
> but if ye, through the spirit, do mortify
> the deeds of the body, ye shall live.
>> Romans 8:12-13

Paul does not give us a simple message of joy and happiness if we follow Christ. Rather, he makes us aware of the spiritual battle we must face if we are to deal with our lives honestly and if we are serious about the quest for a great love. The joy we receive comes from the knowledge that what we do is true and good, thus we develop a spirit of love in the midst of hardship.

Paul understands human nature well enough to know that rather than facing the sin within ourselves we often accuse and judge others. It becomes our almost automatic response to see the speck of dust in our neighbors eye rather than the logjam in our own. This failure to transform ourselves has serious consequences, as Paul warns us:

> But, why dost thou judge thy brother? Or
> why dost thou set at nought thy brother?
> For we shall all stand before the judg-
> ment seat of Christ.
> For it is written, as I live, saith the Lord,
> every knee shall bow to me, and every
> tongue shall confess to God.

> So, then, every one of us shall give account of himself to God.
>
> Romans 14:10-12

By what law are we to discipline ourselves and deal with our internal conflicts? By what principles are we to transform our base selves into something precious? By the spirit of God's love.

We may feel impatient, cruel, jealous, boastful, conceited, selfish, offended, resentful and a host of other emotions within. Paul's response to us would be: We must discipline ourselves, transform ourselves with God's love. We may not like discipline and we may complain that it is not easy to love those who offend us. Paul would, nevertheless, exhort us to follow the true path of love. By studying the *Bible* we can receive a spiritual nourishment as powerful as that from prayer.

It is my observation that when we are spiritually at a low point, when we feel closed and cold in heart, when we don't want to overcome the obstacles within, then the last thing we want to do is to pray or to study the scriptures. Prayer and study confront us with ideals, with the necessity of changing ourselves. When we are reluctant to deal with the difficulty of changing ourselves, we seek to avoid any confrontation with truth, for truth is painful. If prayer and study are done sincerely, however, a force can be set in motion that can make us act in new ways. Action then leads us to solidify the transformation of ourselves.

FOOTNOTES

[1] Kenneth Leech, *Soul Friend* (Harper & Row: San Francisco, 1980), p. 168.

[2] Reverend Sun Myung Moon, "The Importance of Prayer" (New York: HSA Publications, April 15, 1979), p. 7.

Chapter Four

Strategies for Overcoming the Obstacles Within: Part Two

Action: Discipline and Practice

If action follows from prayer and study, then it is an action which expresses love. *Virtus est ordo amoris* writes St. Augustine: virtue is the order of love. If we are to act in a virtuous and loving way then we must order our actions. Order, however, demands discipline and practice, two necessary elements if we are genuinely to break down the barriers within to realize our ideals of love. We order, discipline and practice our actions, moreover, in relation to our ideals.

If we accept the disorder of our emotions, if we accept the frustrations that prevent us from expressing our love, then we usually resist any attempt to discipline ourselves. "I don't want to think about it."

"I'm not in the mood to do it." "Don't tell me what to do." "It's not authentic if I do it out of a sense of duty or discipline—I've got to feel it." These are the typical reactions to the necessity of disciplining ourselves in action.

The religious person is often resented because he lives a disciplined and ordered life in obedience to an ideal or to someone who represents that ideal. This is very threatening to one who is undisciplined. Regular prayer, regular periods for study, practice of service to others—all of these actions characterize the religious life. Commitment and obedience to something greater than the self, no matter what the self feels, is the core of the mature life.

Judao-Christian theology sets forth the idea that the fall of man is an act of disobedience to God. Reverend Moon has elaborated on this concept by explaining that in disobeying God we separate, or fall away from, God's heart, God's ideal and God's viewpoint. He goes on to explain that religious history is a restoration of this disobedience, a re-binding or re-establishing a mature relationship with God. Obedience and self-renunciation are central to this process of restoration. To renounce one's selfish, disordered self and to obey God demands tremendous discipline and practice.

The Lord says to Abraham:

Get thee out of thy country, and from thy

> kindred, and from thy father's house,
> unto a land that I will show thee....
>
> (Genesis 12:1)

Obedience is the condition for gaining possession of the promised land. But this obedience does
not come easy for the Israelites. When they obey,
they are blessed by God and prosper; when they diso-
bey, they are punished by God. The covenant obliges
the Israelites to observe God's law, whether they feel
like it or not. God's law is the overwhelming reality
of life; thus it dims the importance of the obstacles
one feels within to respond to that law. Abraham
must have been tortured within to know that God
wanted him to sacrifice his son. He was ready to
make that sacrifice, however, if he knew that it was
God's will.

A terrible irony today is that many young people feel called to the discipline and service of the religious life, yet their parents resent their choice. As
the parents have been won over to the rewards of the
world, they often block out completely the signals
within that call one to a life of obedience to God. As
long as God calls for two hours worship on Saturday
or Sunday, then there is no problem. But if God demands more, watch out. How would modern parents respond to the following words of the Lord:

> Behold, I set before you this day a blessing
> and a curse:
> A blessing, if ye obey the commandment

of the Lord your God, which I command
you this day;
And a curse, if ye will not obey the commandments of the Lord your God, but
turn aside out of the way which I command you this day, to go after other gods,
which ye have not known.

(Deuteronomy 11:26-28)

God does not demand only external action,
He is just as concerned about our internal attitudes.
If we have lived impure, undisciplined lives, then
we must confront our internal selves and change.
We cannot just go through the motions of prayer,
study and service. We must genuinely awaken our
desire to transform our internal selves, then move
from desire to action:

Wherefore the Lord said, For as much as
this people draw near me with their
mouth, and with their lips do honor me,
but have removed their heart far from
me, and their fear toward me is taught by
the precept of men;
Therefore, behold, I will proceed to do a
marvelous work and a wonder; for the
wisdom of their wise men shall perish,
and the understanding of their prudent
men shall be hidden.

(Isaiah 29:13-14)

In the *New Testament* Jesus explains, in a way similar to that expressed in Isaiah, that obedience to the will of God, not mere external show, is a proof of love: "Not every one that saith unto me, Lord, Lord, shall enter the kingdom of heaven...." (Matthew 7:21) Jesus himself is confronted with situations that agonize him, yet he is always willing to subordinate his will to God's will:

> 'Father....Take away this cup from me; Nevertheless, not what I will, but what thou wilt.'
>
> (Mark 14:36)

We often justify our inability to obey, or to discipline ourselves, by claiming that there is no authority worthy of obedience. The world, we believe, has been ruled by despots, tyrants and dictators, therefore we had best follow our own emotions and desires. All rebellion is a rebellion against authority, and we often feel justified in rebelling as we point out the shortcomings of authority.

Obedience, discipline and practice, however, must first be seen in reference to ideals which give order, meaning and value to our lives. If our ideal of love is real, then we must order ourselves and even redeem authorities that we believe to be corrupt. Ultimately our feelings and our actions have a moral impact upon ourselves. We have the burden of making ourselves beautiful and loving no matter how hateful the authorities around us.

The mind, the heart, the will, the emotions and the body must all be disciplined, trained, if we are to overcome the bad habits of the past and become new people. Our lives are such that we have often developed many bad habits. We may not have used our minds to think about virtue and value in each situation. We may not have trained our hearts to reach out in service to others. Our will and our desire to do good may have been weakened by past failures. We may fulfill our appetites more regularly than our ideals.

A conversion is necessary if we are "to turn" from the undisciplined self to the virtuous self. Every situation, every moment, every relationship becomes a training ground in which we can practice transforming ourselves. The religious life is one of constant awareness, constant training in relation to ideals. Contrary to the belief of secular analysts, who criticize the religious person for the obstinacy by which he seeks to discipline himself, freedom through disciplined love is a central goal of the religious life.

As we learn to discipline ourselves we become people of character. Public-minded, public-hearted people do not appear through random accident. They are trained by healthy cultures and nourished by great ideals. The good citizen, the loving family and the noble civilization all have their foundation in individuals of character: virtuous, noble, dedicated, idealistic and loving human beings. When families and civilizations degenerate, we can often look to the failure of individual character. Good is an active force that is practiced. For as Edmund Burke reminds us, "All that is necessary for the forces of evil to win in the world is for good men to do nothing."

As we develop a life of discipline we become disciples in relation to an ideal. For Christians seeking to follow the life and teachings of Jesus, the cost of discipleship is great, for it is very difficult to live up to such an ideal. Dietrich Bonhoeffer, the Christian theologian who was killed by the Nazis, explains how discipleship to Christ demands a total separation from sin and a commitment to a life of sanctification and holiness.

"Christianity has ceased to be serious about discipleship,"[1] writes Bonhoeffer. Christians look for a cheap grace and an easy discipleship by proclaiming faith in Jesus, their savior. But Bonhoeffer emphasizes the need for life—changing action to follow the profession of faith. The obstacles within us that block us from God's grace and salvation are not removed easily by a profession of faith alone. If the ultimate purpose of God is to establish a holy community, Bonhoeffer goes on to say, "It is necessary for the sinner to be parted from his sin and still live before God."[2]

Reverend Moon often explains how the disciple finds himself in a midway position. He begins to dedicate his life to Christ, he seeks to make his life new, yet he is drawn back to the old life as he encounters the challenges of the new life. It is exactly this midway position, before one has conquered the old way of life, that makes for the confusion that prevents one from realizing a new ideal. Who has dedicated his life to purity, chastity and obedience and not felt the temptations of impurity, promiscuity and disobedience? Milton's Satan says he would rather reign in hell then serve in heaven; Joyce's hero in *A Portrait of the Artist* leaves the Church after saying, "I will not serve." The young disciple in a religious movement encounters an imperfection in his spiritual teacher and says, "I quit."

The first step of discipleship, Bonhoeffer writes, is to cut off from an old way of life.[3] Not only is this difficult for the disciple, it is equally difficult for friends and family of the disciple to accept this change. St. Francis shocked his family as he dedicated himself to a way of life they considered unreasonable. They took him to the civil authorities to shock him back to his senses, but they failed. St. Thomas Aquinas was kidnapped by his mother and his brothers, then he was locked in a tower with a prostitute. The family was not at all happy with Thomas' dedication. Modern disciples to religious movements are sometimes kidnapped by criminals who have been hired by distraught parents, in an attempt to break their faith. These faith-breakers are sometimes successful, for of course it is much easier to break a fragile faith than raise up a pure, trusting and loving human being.

If one reads the *Bible*, however, the necessity of a profound commitment to a radical faith is emphasized repeatedly. "Ye shall be holy; for I, the Lord your God, am holy." (Leviticus 19:2). There is no compromise with God on the question of holiness. When Jesus commands his disciples he says:

> If any man will come after me, let him deny himself and take up his cross, and follow me.
>
> (Matthew 16:24)

Paul continually advises the disciples about the difference between their past and present lives:

> For ye were once darkness, but now are ye light in the Lord.
>
> (Ephesians 5:8)

We may worship Christ for being the way, the truth and the life, but he is urging us to embody the same qualities as he does. As the ultimate guide, teacher, rabbi or soul friend, Jesus represents an authority who can be followed because he embodies the ideals he teaches. Yet even Jesus' authority is mistrusted by the closest disciples, for they have not been able to overcome their own impurities and thus they have difficulty trusting that someone else could. Mistrust of authorities is more often related to one's own untrustworthiness rather than an abuse by authority. When the young disciple loses faith because he says he cannot trust his teacher, it is in my experience a reflection of his own inability to trust himself as a redemptive, loving agent.

The spiritual teacher, or soul friend, is ideally the guide who can lead the disciple through discipline from internal confusion to order, harmony and love. The relation between soul friend and disciple is very much like parent and child. In the Unification Church we refer to the role of "spiritual parent" and "spiritual child." Kenneth Leech, in his book *Soul Friend*, describes the characteristics of a mature spiritual guide. Such a person possesses a spirit of love, experience, learning, discernment and always yields to the Holy Spirit.[4]

Ideally our physical parents should be our spiritual parents, Reverend Moon teaches, and our home should be our place of worship. There is such confusion in the world, though, that someone other than our parent often assumes the role of our spiritual teacher. This relationship of spiritual parent to spiritual child is as complex as physical parent and child. Any unresolved resentment, anger, confusion and hostility in the physical family will often be re-created in the spiritual family.

Anyone in the helping professions, be he teacher, therapist or minister, has experienced the transference of emotions in the helping relationship. The one being helped often has confused emotions toward someone in a position of authority. Those emotions, which usually have a source in one's past relationships, are then transferred to this new relationship. If the person in authority is genuinely helpful, he can clarify the nature of the relationship based on ethical principles without exploiting the one being helped. Thus a framework for clarifying internal confusion is set-up, and new strategies can be set for overcoming the obstacles within.

With discipline, practice and clarity of choice based on ethical principles we are able to enjoy the rewards of discipleship. We have a sense that we are in control of our lives, not victims of environment or of the machinations of others or of our own confused emotions. We are aware that we have a great potential for value and meaning, we sense that the world is valuable and meaningful, and we realize that our potential value becomes actual value as we act wisely.

Acting with wisdom in realizing value, however, does not mean that we will always go around with smiles on our faces. Life is suffering, says Buddha. Take up the cross, says Jesus. To make the world a better place is no easy task. What reward we are guaranteed is that we will be challenged to be the most value we can be for heaven and earth. Further, with proper training, we can realize our fullest, unique value.

We cannot, though, escape the ultimate challenge of God's call for us to perfect our character and to establish His Kingdom of love on earth. Jesus teaches, "Be ye perfect as your Heavenly Father is perfect" and establish the Kingdom on earth as it is in heaven. The Catholic theologian Hans Kung explains the significance of Jesus' words: "Jesus' message and community raised the question of the aim and purpose to which a man will *ultimately* direct his life. Jesus demanded a final decision for God's cause and man's."[5]

Whatever obstacles we feel within ourselves, we are aware of two voices calling us and we must respond. One voice calls from within. It might be called the "moral imperative" voice as it cries out: "I want to feel good; I want to feel happy; I want to feel loved." The second voice calls from without and might be called the voice of the "ethical command": "Love God with all your heart and mind; love your neighbor as yourself; love all things." All people are confronted by both voices, and they must realize their internal desires in relation to external reality.

It may be true that modern man hears these voices but faintly, if at all. We are so busy with getting and spending in the roar of the market place that the still, small voices are inaudible. We develop then a view of human life and society that reflects the confusion of our internal world: life is filled with sound and fury signifying nothing. Modern literature, from the theater of the absurd to the novels about anguish, nausea and nothingness, depicts the confusion of the modern sensibility.

Rather than ordering life according to classical religious principles, the modern spirit becomes protean, like rubber-man, taking any and every shape. Human life takes the form of the mad Stalin, the crazed Hitler, and the Machiavellian Mao or the Walter Mittys of the world living pitifully petty lives while being consumed by desperate desire. Or, rebels there are without causes. Heroes are anti-heroes. Poems do not mean, they just be. We wait for Godot and wonder why we are waiting. Perhaps there is meaning in the waiting. Perhaps not.

Because the modern world offers us reduced value, for our function or utility only, and seems to offer little in the way of transcendent value, we are called upon to reveal only a minute part of what is within us. We cannot even articulate what obstacles we feel within to the full expression of our selves because we do not have a clear image of the self or its purpose.

Ethical Norms for Action

By understanding the Christian challenge, that we have a divine self that seeks to respond to God's call and build a God-centered world, we immediately have an awareness of a self that must be cultivated in particular directions. We must learn to develop love by caring for , nurturing, and serving other human beings as our brothers and sisters, all of whom are part of one human family. As we develop *philos*, the brotherly-sisterly love, we learn to fulfill the role of a mature husband, wife and parent: we learn the meaning of mature conjugal love and parental love. We thus develop our internal nature and potential to the point where we can exhibit altruistic, unselfish love: the *agape*, Christ-like love toward all members of the human family.

At each point in these relationships we are training ourselves in love through ethical norms. As children we cultivate filial piety, respect for parents and elders. As spouses we cultivate fidelity. And as parents we develop responsibility and loyalty toward universal values represented by God's universal love. In the most basic way then, ethical norms are the central strategies by which we develop an unformed nature into a mature, refined self. We learn to respect, value and love the other.

This religious model of growth has markedly different implications than the Marxist model. In Marxism human beings are largely valued for how they participate in the class struggle. Human beings who are not part of the revolutionary class can easily be eliminated, for they are holding back the inevitable will of history. Since human beings do not have a divine or eternal value, as Marxism rests on an atheistic and materialistic world view, they can be killed *en mass* without compunction. Consequently, we find millions killed in Soviet *gulags*, Chinese re-education centers and Cuban prisons.

Even in western, capitalist societies, little

thought is given to the consequences of economic decisions on human dignity and community. If people are truly to develop their potential and exhibit strategies of love, they must participate much more in the economic and political processes that affect their lives.

While many people recognize the need to develop themselves in relation to a religious ideal, they often resent the reality of "institutionalized religion" or the structures of authority that attend religious institutions. All of us, perhaps, have been hurt in some way by a church, synagogue or organized structure of religion. I suppose just as many people have been more hurt by other institutions. We cannot judge something, however, only by its abuse.

The organized structure that defines the ethical norms of a religious life can offer an individual guidance and training through the stages of the developing self. The religious teacher can share experience, wisdom and love while guiding a young person. Religious texts, rituals and work projects train the mind, heart and will. A religious community can be a model of the larger human community where one can learn to become a transforming agent of the larger world.

Religious communities that represent values different from the world are often looked upon with hostility by that world. They are seen as subversive agents. The persecution of Catholics, Mormons, Unificationists and numerous other groups is largely because these groups have established communities to set themselves off from the norms of the world. Members of such communities are accused of having lost their minds, of being under a hypnotic spell of a power-hungry leader and of being victims of various delusions. Rarely does one ask what the community *believes*, for then the questioner would be forced to confront his own worldview. After all, was not Jesus and His community accused of many things, and did not Jesus say essentially that the world was deluded, was following false powers and had lost its real senses?

The Christian challenge is to live life fully as a responsible human being. It is to understand the burden of one's humanity, the divine nature of the self, and the role of the Christ as the central archetype between God and man, man and society, and man and man.

This is a very different concept of self and its fulfillment than that of modern psychology. Many writers describe modern psychology as a kind of religion which worships the self. In Dr. Paul C. Vitz's book, *Psychology as Religion: the Cult of Self-Worship*, he explains the modernist obsession with the self:

> Selfist psychology emphasizes the human capacity for change to the point of almost totally ignoring the idea that life has lim-

its and that knowledge of them is the basis of wisdom. For selfists there seem to be no acceptable duties, denials, inhibitions, or restraints. Instead, there are only rights and opportunities for change. An overwhelming number of the selfists assume that there are no unvarying moral or interpersonal relationships, no permanent aspects to individuals. All is written in sand by a self in flux. The tendency to give a green light to any self-defined goal is undoubtedly one of the major appeals of selfism, particularly to young people in a culture in which change has long been seen as intrinsically good.[6]

The sense of self that Vitz describes has very different implications for growth than the disciplined self in relation to a religious ideal. The former self seeks expression in personal gratification and arbitrary, unsystematic choice. There are no ethical norms of behavior other than what pleases the self. Feelings, moods, emotions and intuition are often the basis for action and value. Confusion and obstacles to action are often taken as valuable states of being, for there is a kind of "moral equivalence" between action and inaction. They both may be equally "good" in terms of the feeling of the self. It is like "feeling" that there is no real difference between the Soviet Union and the United States.

I have sometimes observed a member of my

church get tired or discouraged with the discipline of trying to realize a religious ideal. "I have been trying to overcome this difficulty for five years; I give up". If I point out that with some aspects of the self one never ceases to struggle, there may be even greater discouragement. Following frustration the person begins to develop a new view of the self. "I am alright the way I am. I don"t need anyone to pressure me or make me feel guilty. God can work through me as I am, on my terms."

Reaction to discipline and authority often leads to rationalization of new behavior, rejection of the religious teaching and authority, and usually the embracing of a philosophy of "I am the center of the world." Since a sense of relief, even joy, immediately follows the rejection of authority, the person feels reassured that his new path is the correct one. "It can't be wrong if it feels so right." Further, the person then usually seeks out others who embrace his philosophy of self, and thus a kind of new community of re-enforcement is set up. For example, it is common for apostate members of religion to seek other apostates.

Action: Anxiety, Guilt and Suffering

The feelings of the self then must be expressed either through a process of discipline, obedience and practice or through the joy of unrestrained self expression. Either mode of self expression, however, must come to terms with pain, suffering, anxiety and guilt, which are often the central stumbling blocks to the realization of any value.

When we speak of obstacles within we mean to say obstacles to the realization of value. Human beings, in their nature and essence, are value-seeking and value-making beings. We feel anxiety to create value, for we know that is our purpose in life, and we feel guilty when we fail to realize our full potential for life. Rollo May describes the condition of such a person in the following terms: "...the condition of the individual when confronted with the issue of fulfilling his potentialities is anxiety.... When the person denies these potentialities, fails to fulfill them, his condition is guilt."7

May emphasizes that human beings must take upon themselves the responsibility for choosing values. From the point of view of existential philosophy and psychology, "existence precedes essence," so we must create who we are to be. Through our action we determine our value. Thus May, for example, argues that the feelings of dignity and self-worth come from responsible action. Anxiety is the burden we feel before we take responsibility for creating value. Guilt arises from the failure to choose value that actualizes (is part of) our deepest potential.

May identifies two personality types: the inner-directed and outer-directed. Briefly, the inner-directed person is one who reaches into the deepest part of himself in identifying value. On the other hand, the outer-directed individual is someone who merely takes on fully formed the cloak of identity and value given by an organization. At some point this outer-directed person begins to feel resentment, hostility and self-hatred. Even if what he is doing is in fact very good, he may feel hostile toward that good if he has not identified within himself the need to realize that good.

Within a large corporation, for example, an executive may take on for himself all the elements of corporate culture. From dress code to language to patterns of social behavior he models himself after a company standard. If, however, his deepest nature cannot identify with the values and ideals of the corporate culture, then at some point there is hostility, aggression and a desire to subvert the company.[8]

A young church member may be inspired by the ideals of his church and throw himself completely into the activities demanded by religious commitment. If, however, he has not come to terms with himself and God, the complexity of good and evil, selfishness and unselfishness within his own character, then anxiety may build until there is rebellion against church authority and structure. There may not be anything wrong with church authority and structure, yet there is a reaction by the individual who has not yet identified this value within himself.

Leadership of any organization will always be ready to give directions and orders, and people usually find it satisfying in the short run to be given clarity of purpose and action. If leaders, however, are not sensitive to the unique, complex reality of the individual human being, then there will eventually be a reaction on the part of the one being led. There must be internal as well as external understanding and motivation if individuals are to realize value through action.

Now there are difficulties associated with existential psychology, for the emphasis in creating value is on personal choice. There is little clarity about standards of value and even the concept of human potential is left very vague. Value becomes highly personal and subjective: What is true for me is what I value. Without a clear sense of the essence and nature of a human being the subjective, existential chooser continues to feel anxiety by failing to create integrity and continuity of choice in relation to a real self.

The rigid moralist, on the other hand, adheres to moral principles even though he neither identifies them within his self nor embodies them in action. Such a moralist often has great hostility to ones who violate his moral code, for his own insecure identity is threatened by the challenge of someone with a different code. I have been shocked by the hatred with which some Jewish and Christian groups first responded to the Unification Church in America. Ministers who preach love and tolerance would respond to us with the most vehement bigotry and hatred. Even if they imagined us to be evil, surely their response to us should have been one of love. But no, venomous attacks came upon us without their even seeking to understand, by reading any of our literature or by speaking to us, what we believe and why we do what we do.

From the Unification point of view value lies in our nature and purpose. Since we are both physical and spiritual beings, we have both a physical and spiritual desire. This nature and desire must be expressed or else we feel anxiety and guilt. Since we are created by God, our nature ultimately seeks a relationship to God and God's purpose. If we do not understand God and His purpose, then we are never rid of the most fundamental anxiety about our being. We have a purpose to bring joy to God and joy to the world by developing a heart of love that resembles God's universal and absolute love.

As we develop a relationship with God, through prayer, meditation, study and action, we then realize we also have a relationship to the human community. God's purpose for us is mandated by his commandment to love our neighbor as ourselves. Finally, we are stewards over the environment and we must use all things for the greater glory of God and the well-being of the human community.

We have, consequently, a nature that resembles God and a value potential that is universal, eternal and absolute. We are not blank slates who must create ourselves from scratch. We also are not beings who gain our identity from our function: I am not merely what I do. Unificationism pursues the idea that:

> ...man, in seeking after values and in realization of them, must take into account on the one hand the absolute centrality of God as the source and goal of creation to whom man must bring joy and satisfaction and on the other God's provision of means for man to find, ultimately, absolute truth, goodness, and beauty.[9]

Related to guilt and anguish as potential obstacles to the realization of our ideals are pain and suffering. When we are hurt, when we feel pain, when we sorrow and suffer, then we often become paralyzed and are unable to actualize the potential for great value. We usually react to pain and suffering as evils that we want to avoid or to rid ourselves of them as quickly as possible. We want to drown our sorrows or fight against that which causes us pain. The strategy of the religious person, however, is one where ideally one tries to understand the meaning and nature of suffering and then how to use that suffering to create value. If all things must be used for the greater glory of God, then we must use even our pain and transform it into a value for God. We cannot live without suffering. The question is: What do we do with our suffering?

The modern man's fear of pain and suffering

stems partly from the lack of meaning he perceives in his suffering. Almost daily we read about or experience some situation which is filled with horror, terror or misery. These experiences, however, very rarely lend themselves to affirming any great meaning or value. In this week's New York newspapers we read of an old man shot in a grocery store as he is robbed of three dollars in change; a couple out of work lock themselves in their garage, let their car run and are found dead; a young man writes of how his mother was a bag-lady and how he has found meaning by getting up at five in the morning and painting graffiti on subway cars.

Even much of the great literature of our age expresses the meaninglessness of suffering. Camus' Sisyphus rolls a rock up a hill until he gets to the top, then the rock comes tumbling back down. He is condemned to continue rolling the rock back up the hill. He finds some meaning in the effort and the knowledge that other people are rolling their rocks up hills, but this is precious little meaning for most of us. Ralph Ellison's Invisible Man suffers the misfortune of being a black man in a hostile white society. He suffers and looks for consolation by thinking of the verse in the blues song, "What did I do to be so black and blue." Solzhenitsyn reveals to us the heart of darkness within the ghastly Soviet *gulags* and Elie Wiesel is given the Nobel Prize for literature as he documents for the world the horrors of the Nazi holocaust.

Most people cope with all of this suffering by trying to escape from it. We drug ourselves not only on crack, heroin, cocaine, marijuana, and alcohol, but on food, sex and entertainment. We consume more and more that will allow us to forget more and more. We divert ourselves from the serious business of life through films, football and soap operas. If we don't find the appropriate soporific, if we cannot escape from pain, then we begin to inflict pain on others.

Child abuse, husbands abusing wives, abuse of the elderly, abuse of the environment, abuse of each other, crime against anything and everything and ultimately the abuse and hatred of oneself becomes the mode of the modern culture. Finally, there may be quiet resignation to the reality of pain and the stoic and stolid withdrawal into oneself. We wait fearfully for the final terror; not just the local terrorist, but the global nuclear terror.

A religious person is very much aware of the reality of suffering. Billy Graham writes how "at the heart of our universe is a God who suffers...."[10] and Reverend Moon has preached at great length about the suffering heart of God who has been betrayed by His children. The *Bible* speaks of the earth itself groaning in travail because of the wickedness of men. Anyone, moreover, who has truly tried to love another person knows that love is always accompanied by pain, for it is often either unrequited, rejected or misunderstood.

If we study the *Bible*, however, we realize that suffering can offer great value if used in purposeful ways. Jesus promises

> Come unto me, all ye that labor and are heavy laden, and I will give you rest.
> Take my yoke upon you, and learn of me; for I am meek and lonely at heart, and ye shall find rest unto your souls.
> For my yoke is easy, and my burden is light.
>
> Matthew 11: 28-30

These are not idle words that Jesus speaks, nor are we to take them superficially, for Jesus has suffered greatly. He has been ridiculed, mocked, scorned, abused, rejected and hated. His response: offering God's love and truth to hatred and false charges. Even at the moment of death, when he is being horribly and wrongfully murdered, he cries: "Lord, forgive them, for they know not what they do." Jesus' love is remembered by the world as it continues to triumph over hatred and injustice. We discover in Jesus' love qualities which are of God: eternal, absolute and unchanging. The *Bible*, then, teaches us to use suffering to perfect our love. As sin causes suffering, God calls upon the righteous to suffer in overcoming sin. Sin removes us from God and His love. It makes us faithless, hopeless and loveless people. As we sin we violate trust, we act without hope, and we think about ourselves more than any-

103

one else. Reverend Moon then explains how we must pay an indemnity offering to restore our loving relationship with God. This is his central strategy of love in removing the obstacles between ourselves and God.

Through the process of indemnity an individual sets conditions to restore the original relationship of love between God and oneself. Prayer conditions, fasting conditions, conditions of love and service are offerings to God. There may be suffering in doing these conditions, but if our motivation is to restore a relationship of love, then ultimately these conditions give us meaning and joy.

If, for example, we have insulted or abused a friend, then pain ensues. If we wish to restore this relationship and thus heal the heart, we must offer sincere words or deeds toward restoration. If we offer the words insincerely, joylessly, without love, but only through a formal duty, then there is little likelihood of restoration taking place. Indemnity is ultimately an action to restore a violation of the heart.

When Reverend Moon was unjustly imprisoned in a North Korean concentration camp or an American federal prison, he did not react with hatred and resentment. He responded with prayers, tears and a pledge to God that he would do God's will joyfully no matter what condition of suffering he experienced. The religious person always seeks to transform evil into good and suffering into a triumph of love.

104

Job cries, "When He has tested me, I will come forth as gold." (Job 23:10). David sings, "God is our refuge and strength." (Psalms 46:1). First Peter proclaims, "For even here unto were ye called, because Christ also suffered for us, leaving us an example, that ye should follow his steps." (1 Peter 2:21).

If God, our Father, suffers, if Christ suffers, if the righteous and the saints suffer, how are we to prevent ourselves from suffering if we are dedicated to the ideal of love? The world suffers because of its unrighteousness; the righteous must suffer in seeking to love an unrighteous world. When we are unrighteous we violate our nature, our purpose, and our relationship to the environment, to others and to God. Therefore, to restore these relationships we must make a great effort. This may cause us to feel pain, but through this pain we develop a healing love.

In an analogous way, if we abuse our body and get sick we try to restore the body to its original health. We may need to take medicine or go to the hospital for an operation. The medicine and the operation may be painful, but they are necessary if we are to restore health. Religion is like a medicine, a minister is like a doctor and a church is like a hospital. All of these elements may cause pain and discomfort, but they are usually necessary if the patient is to be restored to spiritual health.

Suffering and pain always hurt; no one likes them. However, they can bring us great meaning, great value and great joy. Our trials can equip us to comfort others and to comfort God. If our attitude and heart are pure, if we prepare ourselves for suffering by prayer, by developing love within our family and by strengthening our relationship to God, then we can triumph over the obstacles within through love. If, however, we react to suffering with cynicism, bitterness and resentment, then we are lost—and the world is lost. God's attitude, as he has witnessed the horrors of human history, has been to embrace the base stuff of the world and transform it, with gratitude and a heart of love, into gold.

FOOTNOTES

1 Dietrich Bonhoeffer, *The Cost of Discipleship* (New York: Macmillan Publishing Co., 1979), p. 98.

2 Bonhoeffer, p. 307.

3 Bonhoeffer, p. 66.

4 Kenneth Leech, *Soul Friend* (San Francisco: Harper & Row, 1977), pp. 88-89.

5 Hans Kung, *The Christian Challenge* (New York: Doubleday & Company, 1979), p.328.

6 Paul C. Vitz, *Psychology as Religion* (Grand Rapids, Michigan: William P. Eerdmans Publishing Co., 1977), p. 38.

7 Rollo May, *The Discovery of Being* (New York: W.W. Norton & Company, 1983), p. 112.

8 See David Halberstam's analysis of Ford and Nissan in *The Reckoning* (New York: William Morrow & Company, 1986).

9 Sebastian Matczak, *Unificationism* (New York: Learned Publications, Inc., 1982), p. 163.

10 Billy Graham, *Till Armageddon* (Waco, Texas: Word Books, 1981), p. 100.

Chapter Five

Strategies for Overcoming
The Obstacles Without

Overcoming the obstacles within ourselves in realizing the ideal of love is very much connected to the reality of the world without. We seek to overcome our own difficulties so that we may more effectively embrace the people and places that make up our world. The real world without, however, may not always allow itself to be embraced, no matter how much it professes the desire for love. We often confront as many obstacles without as we do within. In fact, the world almost mirrors ourselves, with its good and evil, and as we look without we are often frightened by how much we resemble that world. We may feel doubly frustrated by seeing the complexity of realizing our ideals, but we may be doubly victorious if we pursue sound strategies of love.

The Art of Caring

Central to love in its most basic form is the art of caring. If we are to embrace the world, and if it is to allow itself to be embraced, we must express a genuine and sincere care. Often we think of people who care as specialists, people in the "caring profession." We look to teachers, ministers and therapists as ones who are trained to care. But all of us are endowed with the ability, knowledge and experience to be expert caring people. We are all, whether we define ourselves as such or not, teachers, ministers and therapists. Ideally, we can be Christ-like in our ability to draw out love, value and creativity from others as we exhibit these qualities ourselves. We need to train ourselves to develop our skills, but no degree is necessary for us to become Christ-like. What degree did Jesus have other than Son of God?

The school where we first learn to care is our family. Families offer training in almost every conceivable type of caring: caring for those younger or older, caring for the sick or emotionally distraught, caring in times of need or in times of prosperity. We learn as children to care for grandparents, to love and respect parents, and to embrace brothers and sisters. We learn to have compassion for those with short-comings and to encourage those who have failed. We learn the art of listening to the words and hearts of those with whom we live. We learn to speak words of forgiveness, reconciliation and love.

The family is the most ideal school of care and love, yet we still face the larger challenge of applying all we have learned in our physical family to the larger human family. The minister of a church, who may be called Father, or in the case of the Unification

Church we refer to Reverend and Mrs. Moon as Parents, tries to teach the human family about care from God's point of view. "The Pastor," writes Paul Pruyser, "tries to view people through the eyes of Christ, as being on the way to the Kingdom, and see how far they are from it...."[1] Christ looks at the God-like potential within each person and attempts to draw out that potential with patience, care and love. Christ is not blind to sin and imperfection but rather than accusing, judging and hating the sinner he tries to bring about transformation through love.

Too often the parent or the minister is unable to listen deeply. We almost all find it easier to speak rather than to listen, and when we listen we do not listen with our whole heart and soul. Martin Buber speaks of an "I and thou" relationship where subject and object are bound up in mutual care. Buber can even "hear" the voice of a tree. Our listening tends to be not so creative and our speaking, even if we desire to help others, an abstract sermonizing. The minister all too often ministers to his own dogmatic mind rather than to the sensitive soul before him.

Sometimes those people in the "caring professions" are the least caring, as they cultivate a business in lieu of care. "Often, people get on treadmills...like these because there's something they wish to avoid. Some area of their life is fundamentally wrong, but they either don't know how to deal with it or believe they had better not. Consequently, they establish a network of business with themselves at the center and the problem way off in the background just outside their range of vision."[2] Unfortunately, the minister, like the parent, is sometimes the strict disciplinarian rather than the warm, embracing nourisher. The result is often children who are anxious to leave home and church alike.

Many of us run from our homes and churches to find others who care enough to help us. The therapist has become a common parent or surrogate minister. And indeed the therapist will often provide the care that others have failed to provide. Howard Clinebell compares the historical function of the minister with the contemporary role of the therapist. Where the minister has traditionally been concerned with anointing, exorcism, consoling, advice-giving, confession and disciplining, the therapist offers psychotherapy, support counselling, educative counselling and confrontational counselling.[3] Where the therapist may offer a model of health that is consonant with contemporary culture, the minister is more able to offer a path that can resemble God's ideal.

The caring process ideally focuses on what a person can be rather than on what he is not. Renewal and revitalization are goals. If the process is successful, then there is an enhancement of the ability to receive and to respond. Ministry like therapy tries to identify emotional and intellectual blocks to health, then the minister attempts to remove those blocks so an individual can get on with living, loving and working well. If the church is to be effective it must not only proclaim the ideals of the Kingdom, it must also be relevant to the unique human needs of each individual. If the individual does not feel embraced, he will drop out of relationship no matter how noble the ideals.

We may mistakenly take our model of the caring relationship from the T.V. host or hostess who appears to be warm and affable. My experience on many interview shows, however, is that T.V. personalities are just that: personalities rather than sincere, genuine caring persons. On a recent show the hostess, with a constant smile, kept interrupting me and seemed to hear very little when I attempted to answer her questions. We did not have what I consider a real conversation. She pretended interest in the questions she asked while trying to provoke me into some indiscretion. I began thinking more of the audience reaction to my answers than in relating to the hostess.

Often we are frustrated in our care for others because they either forget our concern or need the care again and again. There is, though, no end to the caring relationship. There is no final solution to the needs people have, therefore we must realistically understand how each day will offer new challenges. In fact, I find it most effective for me to anticipate people's needs before they express them. I set for myself concrete goals each day and then try to evaluate how I have fulfilled those goals at the end of a day.

Since I know how all of us like to receive birthday cards, I try to send out cards each month to those people with whom I am in regular contact. I occasionally make "love calls" to various church leaders just to express my concern and my good wishes. I answer mail with reasonable punctuality and try to send along an acknowledgment and an audio tape to letters that need no formal response. I try never to eat by myself but rather to ask someone to join me. By following up relationship in these small ways I try to show that I am committed and dedicated in my caring relations with others. The commitment is one where I pledge to act in ethical and loving ways according to a God-centered standard of value.

I often fail to realize my own ideals, and often others make demands on me that are not in harmony with these ideals. Relationships can break down. I pray each day, however, that I can be forgiven for my failures and that God will give me the strength, wisdom and love to heal relationships that have been treated carelessly.

I am always made aware that through caring relationships I become a change agent, a transforming and enabling person. In reaching out to others I enable them to deepen their own love by responding to me. If someone has been hurt and has become bitter and cynical, they need to encounter someone who can heal, embrace and love. We are bound up in relationship whether we like it or not, and we create either heaven or hell for ourselves by the quality of our relationships.

Friendship

Directly related to caring is the friendship we establish with the other. We sometimes establish friendships for utility or for pleasure, but what a God-centered ideal demands is friendship based on an ideal of the good. The needs for friendship and love are rooted in our nature and our desire, but they must be directed toward the good if they are to endure. Friendships can break down easily if they are not based on the values inherent in the whole person, and the desire to seek altruistically the benefit, welfare and happiness of the other.

Aristotle writes in *The Nicomachean Ethics:*

> Perfect friendship is the friendship of men who are good, and alike in virtue; for these wish well alike to each other *qua* good, and they are good in themselves. Now those who wish well to their friends for their sake are most truly friends; for they do this by reason of their own nature and not incidentally; therefore their friendship lasts as long as they are good— and goodness is an enduring thing.[4]

Often we consider as friends those who do

something tangible for us in our quest for pleasure or utility, and we feel we have no friends when we appear to get no tangible good out of the relationship. But friendship, like care and love, may not always involve pleasing moments that we perceive as good. A true friend may often tell us things that are unpleasant to hear, but they are true and necessary for us to hear. Leaders of all types, for example, are surrounded by flatterers and sycophants who wish to ingratiate themselves with the leader and care little about an ideal of the good.

"Friendship is always a sweet responsibility, never an opportunity," writes Gibran. Like care and love, friendship demands genuine, responsible commitment to the other. Only in this way can friendship grow, mature and exhibit its full value. For like all things of value, friendship needs a process of time by which it can ripen.

Furthermore, friendship like love demands an ability to seek the benefit of the other even at one's own expense. Jesus exclaims that the greatest friendship is the giving of one's own life for a friend. Friendship and love are inextricably bound together, for one can not be a true friend without love. Pope John Paul II writes: "Man's capacity for love depends on his willingness consciously to seek a good together with others, and to subordinate himself to that good for the sake of others, or to others for the sake of that good."[5]

When I first began to deepen my commitment to God and the religious life, I found that some friendships from the past began to weaken, and I noticed a kind of resentment from those with whom I used to spend much time. I did not feel any hatred toward the past, but rather I shared my newly deepened religious commitment with those I felt close to. If this commitment was not shared, then I had to make a conscious choice as to what kind of friendships and relationships I desired. I turned toward more value-oriented and, for me, more genuine friendships based on ideals of service and love of God.

Recently, a young woman of college age began coming to our church. She studied our theology and enjoyed the fellowship with members of our church. After a period of time she began to spend more and more time involved with church activities. The boyfriend with whom she had been living resented her new commitment and tried to dissuade her from participating in what to him were activities of little value. She could not be dissuaded. The boyfriend then went to her parents and to ministers of other churches and told all kinds of horrible stories about how we had captured this innocent young lady. The lady's choice of new friendship caused her much pain and our church received hostile criticism. The root of the problem was the boyfriend's jealousy in the light of his friend's commitment to values he did not share.

In the case of this young man, he sought pleasure from his girlfriend and was not genuinely concerned with any good beyond his own personal pleasure. No one ever proclaims that the love or friendship he offers is false. However, if we have a broad framework for genuine value, we can observe how much love and how many friendships are based on pure emotional pleasure. Such relationships may involve much intensity, nevertheless they are often shallow in terms of value. Pope John Paul II points out that trust, peace and joy come from love based on virtue; suspicion and jealousy come from love based essentially on desire.

Emotion and desire are mercurial as the basis for relationship, especially in terms of erotic or sexual attraction. We are often attracted to someone based on an instinctual urge, but if our attraction is not based on an ideal of the good, relationships can easily be destructive. Many religions have prohibitions against premature sexual relations because they recognize that a person is more than desire, and moral codes are necessary to guide a person to full human maturity. "Sexual morality comes into being not only because persons are aware of the purpose of sexual life, but also because they are aware that they are persons."[6]

When we hate someone we essentially see no value in them. We do not care for or about them because we see nothing in them to care about, therefore it is very easy to remove ourselves from relationship

117

with them. Being a Unificationist, I have experienced being the object of such hatred. Although the Unification Church has now established friendship and respect with most religious communities, there is one group in the United States that continuously and consistently seeks to discredit us. Ironically, this group has received terrible persecution in its own history, yet it is now persecuting us in similar ways. The leaders refuse to meet with me or dialogue with our church or answer any letters or telephone calls. They would rather believe that we are of no value and therefore their hatred can be pure and absolute.

If we do not hate others yet still feel alone, we may be people who do not extend friendship. The magazine section of *The New York Times* not long ago had a cover story about being alone in America. While many Americans feel alone, cut off from others, they often do not feel responsible for initiating caring relationships. Since we are all hurt at one time or another, we often justify our inability to reach out by saying that we tried and were rebuffed. We are all, however, caught in the essential dilemma of life: we cannot feel fully cared for unless we offer the fullness of ourselves to the other.

Robert Bellah and his associates did a recent study of individualism and commitment in American life and found that this inability to care for the other was a source of much breakdown in marriages:

Americans believe in love as the basis for

enduring relationships. A 1970 survey found that 96 percent of all Americans held to the ideal of two people sharing a life and a home together. When the same question was asked in 1980, the same percentage agreed. Yet when a national sample was asked in 1978 whether 'most couples getting married today expect to remain married for the rest of their lives,' 60 percent said no. Love and commitment, it appears, are desirable, but not easy. For, in addition to believing in love, we Americans believe in the self. Indeed... there are few criteria for action outside the self. The love that must hold us together is rooted in the vicissitudes of our subjectivity. No wonder we don't believe marriage is easy today.[7]

Even in our work we may find it difficult to care for others or to be committed to our organization. We may learn to win or lose on the corporate battlefield, but rarely do we learn to become full caring and loving persons. A plethora of books lament how individuals at work feel exploited, used and discarded by the market place, like the products they produce. Economic decisions do not often consider the dignity of the worker and how decisions will affect the human community. Perhaps Japan is now more successful in corporate competitiveness with the United States because of the treatment of employees. In many Japanese corporations the employee feels that he, his family and the well-being of his nation are of great concern to the management. Consequently, employees feel ethically bound to quality work for their corporation.   •

Paul Goodman, the social critic, warned Americans in the 1950's and 1960's that a generation was growing up absurd. He lamented the shoddy, built-in obsolescence of many products. He pointed to the alienation felt by many employees. He inspired young people to seek to fulfill their human nature in work, not merely to seek status and wealth.

Reverend Moon has often spoken about why Jesus always seems so lonely and has so few friends. To be a friend to Jesus demands much: total commitment and responsibility for building God's Kingdom of love. Jesus sets the standard of true care and true friendship. We must love each other as we would love God, and to love our Father we must do His will. Reverend Moon explains that we each have divine value, universal value and cosmic value in potential. We must, however, draw out this value from each other through caring and loving relationships. A commitment is necessary each moment to make others, and thus ourselves, valuable, and thus we become true friends.

Virtue

The pressures, stresses and difficulties of life are thus made clear. We are condemned to be free;

we feel committed to love; we have the potential for great value; we feel the difficulty of realizing that value; we want to escape from freedom. Finally, we must choose to be virtuous, or not.

Alexander Pope writes: "Know this truth (enough for man to know), Virtue alone is happiness below." All culture sets up ideals of "the good": objectives worthy of desire and action defined by standards of ethics and value. When a culture becomes confused about its "goods", or when it has specious or minimal goods, it collapses. The Unification world view sets forth goods not just for a particular culture but for the world. It sets forth a framework for God-centered ethics and ideals and offers a pattern for the individual to exhibit virtue in terms of this framework. It emphasizes that each individual is responsible to know the truth (right goals and right ways for our desire and action) and to practice it. If we do so, then we become people of virtue (from the Latin *vir*, meaning human) who can give hope to the world.

In contemporary American culture there seems to be great confusion as to the nature of any good; consequently, even the concept of virtue seems archaic, not to speak of the practice of it. Americans are asking the basic questions of who they are and how they should relate to each other. What is a man? What is a woman? What is a marriage? What is a family? Should I develop my head, my heart, my body, or all three? Recently I had lunch with a bril-

121

liant scholar who lamented that he was unable to embrace his son. Childless women who have been high achievers in business are now finding there is something missing in their lives. Children in school are taking harder drugs and suffering from alcoholism, drug addiction and venereal disease. We look to Dear Abby columns and the Johnny Carson show as sources of wisdom, morality and virtue.

Historically, the great cultures have emphasized the need to understand clearly the nature of the good and then to develop strategies to realize that good. The Old Testament sets forth a law to be followed by the Hebrew people. As Psalm One tells us, if they follow the law they will prosper, if they violate the law they will suffer. Moreover, the heroes and heroines of the Old Testament are models of virtue. Moses, Joshua, Daniel, Ruth and Esther exhibit faith, courage, fidelity and love in embodying the law. For the Hebrews, every area of life involves a moral choice, and they feel chosen by God to be an example of virtue in a world of darkness.

The Greek ideal of the good and virtuous person was similar to the Hebrew ideal. The Greeks believed that the world was ordered in a rational way and that it was incumbent upon them to develop reason to understand the world and thus to act in pursuit of real goods. Although there were sophists who taught people about "success" and the strategies to achieve specious goods such as success or power, the best of Greek thought was dominated by philosophers like Socrates. He believed that one must seek truth, real goods, even at the cost of one's life, and he taught that the failure to live well was due to ignorance of such goods. Aristotle taught that each moment we must choose the greater good over a lesser good, then by ordering our life through an integrated pattern of choice we would become virtuous people.

In the *New Testament* Jesus recognizes that many people had fallen away from God and a clear standard of value. Among many of his functions Jesus comes as a standard, or pattern, by which people could embrace the greatest good. He implores people to believe him, to trust him and to follow him. He says, "I am the way, the truth and the life." He urges people to love the world as he loves the world.

Christian theologians, for example, like Greek philosophers, practiced a very concrete strategy of love in seeking to provide a way to realize the ideal of Christian love. They understood human nature and human psychology and recognized that the intellect, the emotions and the will needed to be trained and guided. Through reason and logic the mind could be trained to understand truth; through temperance the emotions could be disciplined to sort out real goods from specious pleasures; through actions demanding strength and fortitude, the will could be trained to overcome pain and difficulty in acts of courage on behalf of justice.

Throughout western culture the Christian

ideal of virtue is presented in literature, art and philosophy. Chaucer, for example, in the "Prologue to the Canterbury Tales" sets forth the description of the Knight:

> A Knight ther was, and that a worthy man,
> That fro the time that he first began
> To riden out, he loved chivalrie.
> Trouthe and honour, fredom and courteisie
>
> . . . .
> And though he were worthy, he was wys
> And of his port as meeke as is a mayde.
> He nevere yet no vileynye ne sayde
> In al his lyf unto no manere wight
> He was a verray, parfit, gentil knight.

At the center of Unification ethics is God, whose essence is heart, purposeful love, and who is the subject of love and goodness. At the center of human nature we find a corresponding heart that motivates us to think, feel and act for the sake of good. Human ethics involves then a God-centered love in which we seek to love based on God's purpose, will and desire. Since the family is the base for the realization of the love of God, ethics should be established on the basis of heart among family members. As described previously, in the family we can develop our heart from one of respect for elders to the altruistic love of parents. Family ethics are the basis for social, business and world ethics. In the family we learn to treat people as brothers and sisters and thus develop a way to establish a truly caring human family.

From the Unification point of view, we must understand our nature and purpose if we are to develop strategies of value and love. If we look at ourselves we find that we are beings with a dual nature and a dual desire. We have an internal nature that desires what we may call spiritual values: truth, beauty, goodness and love. We also have an external nature that desires material values: food, clothing and shelter. Corresponding to our nature and desire we have a dual purpose. We are an object to God and need to fulfill God's purpose and desire. Further, we are subject over the creation and need to become fruitful in relationship to the creation as we fulfill our own desire. So, man needs to exhibit value to God while also seeking value for himself.

The central difficulty for man, given this framework of relationship, is how to balance God's purpose with his own purpose. Reverend Moon points out how Jesus realizes absolute value because he aligns God's purpose with his own individual purpose. Since God's purpose is to seek the well-being of the entire human community, the man of greatest value will devote as much of his life as possible for the benefit of others. Reverend Moon writes:

Goodness is acting for the benefit of other

> people. The motive of any good individual, good family, or good society is to do things for the sake of others.... God's definition of goodness is total giving, total service and absolute unselfishness. You live for others and others live for you. God lives for man and man lives for God. Husband lives for wife and wife lives for husband. Here, unity, harmony and prosperity abound.[8]

The goal of the Unification movement is to establish an ethical world centered on God's love. We recognize that no state can make a man morally virtuous; however, it can provide the conditions by which people can more easily choose virtue. At this point in the history of our movement we seek to revitalize society by clarifying the nature and purpose of human life in relation to every area of human culture. When we are involved with projects that deal with art, media or economics, we are not setting up "front" groups to hide the Unification movement; rather we are following our calling in exhibiting strategies of love for each discipline.

By developing strategies of love, we do so upon the fundamental belief that God is the source of love and the source of the good. By loving others we show how we are created in His image, exhibit His nature and thus we become truly good. If we are going to overcome the obstacles to love that confront us in the world, we must develop strategies of care, friendship and ethics, for these are the quintessential strategies of love, and they are the means by which we become virtuous people.

The Community of Faith

Fortunately, we do not have to develop our strategies in isolation. Not only do we each have families who can help us, if we work together with other families we begin to establish a community of faith and love. In the past, religious communities often isolated themselves from the secular world as much as possible. They understood that to re-enforce their value commitments they needed to remove themselves, as much as possible, from the false values of the secular world. Unfortunately, as these communities removed themselves from the larger world they limited their impact on that world, although they may have been able to preserve their own integrity.

The Unification ideal of a community of faith, one in which individuals can develop care, friendship, ethics and thus the strategies of love, must exist within the larger community. Such a community is referred to as a "Home Church." Reverend Moon encourages every member to develop a Home Church community with 360 families in proximity to his own dwelling. The Church member will seek to establish friendship, a caring relationship with his neighbors, and a loving, prayerful commitment to them. In return, he will seek to stimulate a similar response from them. Such is the process of establishing communities of faith in the 137 countries where the Unification movement exists.

If in democratic societies, with tremendous mobility and emphasis on individual achievement, there is no clear ethic or ideal that allows for communities of faith, then individuals feel less responsible to serve and to love others. In "Alone", *The New York Times Magazine* article mentioned earlier, Louise Bernikow writes: "'People no longer have communities to which they are irrevocably tied,' one sociologist explains, 'Communities are brittle, fragile, with a tremendous turnover.' Throughout the country, he finds, 'there is an element of loneliness not far below the surface.'"[9] Such communities, like those in New York City or in any other major city in the United States, become ones of fear and indifference. It is more likely that an individual living within a community such as this will think of survival rather than love.

Mobility is not the problem in itself, for communist societies are often highly stable, yet they do not promote communities dedicated to strategies of love. Members of such communities in communist countries are often victims of coercion, and they too become creatures of fear and indifference. A *New York Times* reporter describes how "For North Koreans, Spontaneity Is in Short Supply":

On the train to Pyongyang from the border town of Sinuiju, across the Yalu River from China, a middle-aged Korean in the dining car, inhibitions loosened by the local beer, offers a toast to the visitors and later visits them in their compartment. Thirty seconds after he enters, an attendant yanks him away to away to a compartment several doors down and closes the door, after which muffled voices and protests can be heard for the remaining two hours of the journey.[10]

Love is premised on the ideal of freedom, and in societies where there is no freedom, where individuals' rights do not exist except as a function of the rule of a dictator, there can be no genuine love beyond the very personal. Communities of faith are not communities of coercion.

The Home Church ideal is that of the caring, creative community centered on God's purpose, value and love. Unification members, as imperfect as we are, seek to establish model families and communities, wherever we live, so that we can become catalysts for change of the larger human community. We look at the founder of our movement as an example of someone who exhibits strategies of love no matter how difficult the external obstacle. When he was unjustly imprisoned in a North Korean concentration camp or an American federal prison, his attitude was the same: be grateful and love others. In both prisons he gained disciples.

Establishing a caring community is difficult inside or outside a prison. In many ways the world is a prison: people are locked inside their fears, prejudices and hatred. As a faith community Unification church members have fasted, prayed and sacrificed for others in an attempt to build loving relationships. The response on the part of the public has often been bewilderment and suspicion about the motivation of such people. Why in the world would anyone dedicate himself sacrificially for the sake of others? Surely, there must be devious ulterior motives.

Praying, fasting and serving others may also not be adequate in convincing others of sincerity or love. Often, the religious person is insensitive to the unique needs of another person, uncomprehensive in communicating love, and just plain foolish in making mistakes. I still remember the horrified look of a lady who attended one of our church luncheons. She was offered a sandwich and coffee, then one of our church members reached over to her coffee, placed sugar in her cup and began to stir it. This was like the boy scout who led the elderly lady across the street, even though he found out too late that she did not want to cross the street.

Because we make mistakes and plan bad strategies of love, we often want to give up the undertaking altogether. We forget the vision, then we withdraw. We may physically live in a community yet spiritually withdraw from others. We may find what pleases us, then limit our commitment to others. We may lose the redemptive heart or imagination to serve the community. Finally, we are confronted with the realization that the private good and the public good must be realized in community. There is no escape from God, from others, or from our true nature. We must be responsible for developing our strategies of love even when we fail.

Life as Art

In a very real sense we are called to be artists with life as the medium for our art. We each have love and imagination by which to transform our experience of reality, and we can practice each day at making our experience finer and more beautiful. Just as art is often an imitation and recreation of life, life itself can consciously become a work of art. Art can have a central theme which gives unity, and an organization of form that reveals harmony and radiance. On the other hand, art can have no unity, little harmony, much confusion and dullness. The artist must deepen his own heart, intellect and sensibility before he can create something of great meaning and beauty.

If the story of our life is a tale told by an idiot, full of sound and fury, signifying nothing, then we are still challenged to tell this tale in a beautiful way. Beauty itself signifies something. The story told well, like the life lived well, can transform cruelty and indifference into something beautiful and comforting. The classical writers believed that art had two primary functions: to please and to teach, *dulce et utile*. Even tragedy, Aristotle explained, could arouse in us pity, fear and terror, yet we could be cleansed of these emotions and perceive something beautiful and truthful about life if the work of art exhibited aesthetic principles.

Like art, the two primary functions of life, I would argue, are to please and to teach, to offer love and truth. To be loving and truthful is no guarantee that we will be joyful and live a life of comfort. On the contrary, given the world as it is a life of love and truth will almost certainly bring down upon oneself the wrath of the world. However, the integrity and the beauty of such a life well lived is a consolation devoutly to be wished, for it is pleasing to God.

This is why the story of Jesus is said to be the greatest *story* ever told. It is also the greatest life ever lived. It is a story that must be told again and again. It is a story of great suffering, great love, great beauty, offering us great comfort and consolation. I feel, upon hearing the story of Jesus, that love and the beauty of life well lived can triumph over death itself.

Creativity and love lie dormant within ourselves; they await to be awakened by the teacher, the minister, or the caring person. We must help each other become artists of life by stimulating what is best within us. I have been a volunteer worker in a psychiatric hospital, a federal prison and a home for elderly people. In each of these institutions I have encountered very lonely, sad people. Yet, I invariably found that they would respond in creative and beautiful ways if I would read to them poetry or short stories.

The creative and loving heart that lies within each of us is the revolutionary force that drives human culture. Like the artist, each of us can become a revolutionary who turns from what is to what can be. The world may not be filled with happiness, love, value, purpose, and courage. However, we can draw out these qualities from others if we plan wisely our strategies of love.

Just as we must practice every day, we may have failures every day before we make great breakthroughs. Thomas Edison, it is said, experienced 10,000 failures before his phonograph record began playing "Mary Had a Little Lamb." Reverend Moon has written:

> Up to the present time, people have thought religious life belonged to some airy plane far above human life, and imagined that God would just sweep them away to Heaven with His power. But the way to Heaven is to broaden the scope of our love by loving the people in our homes, by loving our neighbors, our fam-

ily relatives, the whole population of the world.[11]

Love is the divine gift that God gives each of us. A life of love is not only the supreme art, it is a witness to the world of God's transforming power. Everyone's life is a witness to something. The question posed to us is whether we want our witness to be to something trivial or to something grand.

FOOTNOTES

[1] Paul W. Pruyser, *The Minister as Diagnostician* (Philadelphia: Westminster Press, 1976), pp. 60-61.

[2] Herbert J. Freudenberger, *BurnOut* (New York: Doubleday, 1980), p. 126.

[3] Howard J. Clinebell, Jr. *Basic Types of Pastoral Counselling* (Nashville: Abingdon, 1966), p. 39.

4 Aristotle, *The Nicomachean Ethics* (Oxford: Oxford University Press, 1980), p. 196.

5 Karol Wojtyla, *Love and Responsibility* (New York: Farrar, Straus, Giroux, 1981), p. 29.

6 Wojtyla, *Love and Responsibility*, p. 33.

7 Robert Bellah, et.al., *Habits of the Heart* (Berkeley: University of California Press, 1985), p. 90.

8 Reverend Sun Myung Moon, *A Prophet Speaks Today*, ed. W. Farley Jones (New York: HSA-UWC Publications, 1975), p. 19.

9 Louise Bernikow, "Alone" *The New York Times Magazine* (August 15, 1982), p. 26.

10 John F. Burns, "For North Koreans, Spontaneity Is in Short Supply," *The New York Times* (July 10, 1985), p. A8.

11 Reverend Sun Myung Moon, *A Prophet Speaks*, p. 57.

Chapter Six

Strategies for Overcoming
The Obstacles Without: Part Two

Limited Definitions of Love

Central to any strategy of love in overcoming obstacles is the recognition that love itself is the most powerful, transforming force. But love presents us with a dilemma. We have the potential within us to express a great love, for we can love the world as God loves the world, yet we must choose to activate that force. We exhibit our freedom if we choose to fulfill our potential for love, or we can escape from freedom by giving and receiving a lesser love. If we are challenged with a standard of love that is defined as God's love, true love, then we must respond to this ideal or react.

Often our definition of love is limited. "I love my car" or "I love the New York Mets" are expressions that indicate the pleasure we derive from something, but perhaps our dedication to these things is very limited. Sometimes I will counsel a couple who say they love each other. Unless they bring God into their definition, what they usually mean is that they are pleasurable to each other. Certainly the failures of love based on limited concepts of the ideal love are among the greatest obstacles to the realization of love.

In many helping relations, for example, love is misused and exploited. A *New York Times* article entitled "Sex With Therapist Said to Harm Client" reveals the obvious destructive consequences of the abuse of love:

> An investigation into the effects of sexual relations between psychotherapists and their patients has found that such intimacy is damaging to at least 90 percent of the patients involved, sometimes resulting in despondency, loss of motivation, exacerbation of the patient's alcoholism or other drug dependency, hospitalization and even suicide.[1]

In this example an authority, here a therapist, like a parent, teacher or minister, who is meant to help someone become a more loving person actually harms the person. Because love is not centered on an ethical, God-centered ideal, but rather on how pleasure can be exploited for personal gain, no transformation can take place. Love either heals or hurts, transforms or deforms.

Abuse by parents, ministers, teachers and counselors makes for the greatest obstacles to the realization of an ideal love. There has been so much false love that many people will not trust that true love is a possibility. Many people do not want to create families or raise children because they themselves have experienced the traumas of an unhappy upbringing. The oppressiveness and insensitivity of ministers has discouraged many people from finding value in "organized religion." They often opt for disorganized, personal religion. The classroom itself is often an arena for shame and judgment, so many people seek to hide their real selves in such an environment.

A number of years ago I taught in an inner-city college where students were often the victims of broken families, oppressive ministers and judgmental teachers. I remember one class just before Christmas where we were to share stories, songs and poems about Christmas. I began by reading Dylan Thomas' "A Child's Christmas in Wales," then I distributed home-baked cookies to the class. No response to the reading or the cookies. The class continued with a Scrooge-like atmosphere of silent response until dismissed. I felt a terrible sadness as I left the room, for I realized that the furthest thing from that classroom was the spirit of Christ's love. I could confront students with the joyful ideals of Christmas, but they could only respond with the painful reality of their past experience.

Many times my own love was tested by my students, for I was challenged to love even when I experienced no response from them. Only through prayer each day in my office before class could I ask God to give me a pure love that would never be discouraged. A great obstacle to the realization of love is to be in an environment that is unloving; it is then that we fear that we do not have the strength to maintain our own love. James Fraser discusses this feeling in a poem entitled "Apprehension":

> I do not fear
> To walk the lonely road
> Which leads far out into
> The sullen night. Nor do
> I fear the rebel, wind-tossed
> Sea that stretches onward, far,
> Beyond the might of human hands
> Or human loves. It is the
> Brooding, sharp-thorned discontent
> I fear, the nagging days without
> A sound of song; the sunlit
> Noon of ease; the burden of
> Delight and—flattery. It is
> The hate-touched soul I dread,
> The joyless heart; the unhappy
> Faces in the streets; the
> Smouldering fires of unforgiven
> Slights. These do I fear. Not
> Night, nor singing seas, nor
> Rebel winds. But hearts unlovely,
> And unloved.

The way to overcome this fear is through mobilizing the resources of the spiritual life: prayer, study, and service to others in spite of one's fear.

Often as we change our physical and spiritual environment, we forget the basic principles of the spiritual life that are necessary to power us over new obstacles. A missionary in our church may move from a small town in the Northwest to New York City. Perhaps the streets in New York are dirtier, people less friendly, church work less nourishing or supportive, regularity of prayer and care more complicated. I will sometimes hear that such a person is struggling spiritually because the new mission "is too much to handle". The missionary may not reach out to me even if I know him well; he may begin to isolate himself in his room; he may begin to imitate the cynical, skeptical and sarcastic tone of people around him.

In such a position we are thrown back on ourselves—and God—and must begin to take initiative to reconstruct the healthy spiritual life. God's love can be the transforming force to make a heaven of the hell we perceive around us. But we must be the activator and the director of that force. We can make ourselves larger by confronting the new challenges with all of our resources, or we can find some small arena for pleasure and escape a larger demand.

Escape, however, has its consequences. If we feel unloved and in an unloving environment, we still have the need for a great love, and so we can develop a pattern of resentment. We begin to complain, to bad-mouth others who we feel are not giving us what we need, and to be jealous of those who are receiving or who can create love.

Love as Authentic Relationship

In order to be effective, we must be aware of the nuances and specific ways we can express love. Love involves awareness of methodology, of how it can be given and received to be effective. Mere words about love or sermons promoting the ideals of love may not bring about the reality of love. We may shout from the pulpit or admonish from the living room easy chair, but if we are unaware of how love is actually given or received we may generate more resentment than love.

It is appropriate to communicate love to a child in one way, to an adolescent in a second way and to an adult in still another way. Still, all children, adolescents and adults are different. We must be sensitive to the needs of particular, unique individuals. This demands that we enter into genuine relationship with the one we seek to love. If we just dump platitudes on the head of the other, we may in fact be avoiding authentic loving relationship. Therefore, it is easier for the insecure parent to yell at his child, or the immature minister to heap fear, guilt and scorn on the congregation, than to enter into secure, genuine giving-and-receiving relationship with the other.

141

If we focus on what a person is not, in our desire to love him, rather than what a person can be, we may crush the one we want to love. Perhaps the recipe for love should be nine parts raising-up through genuine appreciation and praise, one part raising-up through admonition. It is certainly easier to judge someone by an ideal of love, that even we do not represent, rather than embracing the whole person while gently separating out the part that is unlovable. We must love the sinner while hating the sin.

Surely, judgment has become a wholly negative term in the English language because it implies criticism without desire to love. Jesus warns us to judge not, lest we be judged, for he is aware that we are in the world neither to judge others nor ourselves. The ideal of the family is the best arena in which we can evaluate loving criticism in contrast to judgment. The parents in a family must nourish, support and embrace each other as well as seek to offer these qualities to children, whom they must raise up. Family members must have heart, a commitment to love each other, and an ideal of love. When criticism is offered it ideally comes within this larger framework.

Recently in our church an elder member passed away. As the president of the church I was asked to offer a eulogy at the memorial service. Since I did not know the man very well, I called people who did know him and asked them about his outstanding qualities. One person said, "He taught me how to love." Another person commented, "I will miss him, for he showed respect, kindness and genuine care to each person he met." I mentioned these comments in the eulogy, as I realized they were things that could be said of few people, and they were the most important things that religion could offer to anyone.

In a church, as in a family, we may have ideals for ourselves and for others. We may value love, selflessness, knowledge, sensitivity, and understanding. Yet we often encounter resentment, selfishness, ignorance, insensitivity and intolerance. Rather than judging others from our own viewpoint we need a different strategy. We need a plan for redemption that focuses on God's viewpoint and God's desire, not our own. It is often helpful to role-play someone else if we are to understand their viewpoint.

If someone comes to me, for example, and complains about someone else, I will sometimes ask him to do the following exercise: Close your eyes. Imagine that you are the loving parent of yourself and the person you dislike. Now, imagine you are the loving God looking at you and the person you dislike. Ask yourself what kind of changes in your attitude and behavior the parent and God would want from you. Speculate on how you might bring about this change in behavior. As we distance ourselves from our own viewpoint and emotions we are able to perceive from a broader perspective.

I often use this technique to transform my own feelings and attitude. Several weeks ago I returned to the Church headquarters in New York after a trip abroad. As I entered my apartment I wanted to re-place a book on my bookshelf when I saw, to my hor-ror, that all the books in the apartment had been re-arranged. A friend who had been staying with me had decided to arrange the books in what he believed would be a more useful order. I had known where every book was, but now the arrangement made no sense to me. I could imagine myself trying to prepare for a sermon while desperately searching for the book I needed.

As I entered the bedroom and felt the anger reddening my cheeks, I began to think about my teenage son, and I wondered how I would feel if he had rearranged my books. Certainly I would be dis-pleased at first, but I would have to love him for his motivation and effort. I then began to transfer those loving feelings from my son to my friend. I realized how he was trying to care for me through his action, not to diminish me. All of my anger disappeared as I began to imagine the joy of discovering each book anew.

Just as the artist changes our perspective on re-ality as we imaginatively enter into the world of the work of art, so we can all be artists as we use our imagination to transform reality with the primary colors of love. If we constantly focus on the prosaic nature of reality, with all its blemishes and shortcomings, rather than the transforming ideal of love, then we begin to lose hope and the power of the imagination to transform reality. The poet often identifies himself with the priest because he knows that in art, as in religion, the imagination is the bridge between the real and the ideal. Without imagination we do many cruelties in the name of love. Since we almost always deal with people and situations that are not ideal, we must constantly renew our ideals and our love.

Although transforming relationship through love is difficult, because it involves awareness of the self and sensitivity to the other, many strategies can be used to overcome the difficulties. There are, for example, thousands of ways we can validate and acknowledge other people each day. Loving thoughts, kind words and caring actions are always appropriate. It is essential to make time for these simple things, even though we often think we only have time for "more important business."

I detest the phrase "I'm very busy," or actions by people who make me feel they have no time for relationship, no time to answer letters or telephone calls, and no time for being on time for meetings. The people I have found to be the most authentic, and also the most effective, are ones who are always very busy, but who make me feel they have all the time in the world for relationship.

Love demands quality relationship. Quality comes as we give the best of ourselves to the other, even if the giving is in receiving. Very few people feel that they are genuinely listened to; consequently, conversations are often one-way monologues, rather than dialogues. Meaning in relationship comes not just from the content of our words, but from the care of our heart and our commitment to the well-being of the other.

Each time I attend a meeting or meet with someone, I pray that God's spirit of love can work through me so that I can enhance the value of the one I meet. If a couple has difficulty and comes to me for counseling, I usually ask them a simple question: What specific things do you do each day to enhance the value of your spouse? A silence follows. When I ask them if they often pray for the welfare of the other, there is a minimal response. I then give them a homework assignment: During the following week do three specific things for your spouse each day. At the end of each day write down what you have done and bring in the list next week. At the end of a week they are usually startled at their change of attitude and behavior toward their spouse. Obviously, solving the difficulties of relationship is more complex than this exercise suggests, but the principle of doing for the other first remains the same.

THE OBSTACLES WITHOUT: PART 2

Everyday, to each person we meet, we have to say, "I love you" in some new way. Our challenge is to find the strategies that allow us to express the new way. The challenge is one similar to that faced by the singer or song writer. Most songs are love songs, but the love must be expressed in new ways. Even if the song is sung again and again, it must be sung with a new heart and a new enthusiasm. The good singer has a large repertoire, he can move from "Be My Love" to "All You Need is Love."

Reverend Moon has said that "The greatest contribution we can make to the world is to knit all mankind together with the love of God." We can be the supreme artists of life if we create something that is a witness to God's transforming power of love. Every day, however, we are confronted with transforming and re-creating our reality. This is very much our existential dilemma, in that the quality of our existence is determined by the quality of our actions. To be fully human then, we must realize fully the divine love within us. By taking responsibility for our lives, by actualizing our love fully, we solve the dilemma of life and become authentic human beings.

One might argue that life's dilemmas are more complicated than actualizing the divine love within us. Indeed, life confronts us with personal and complex social problems. However, the ideal of love guided by a profound ethic allows us to deal most effectively with each problematic area. In a recent Gallup poll Americans were asked what they most wanted. They responded, in order of importance: (1) personal fulfillment; (2) to be part of a caring group; (3) to do social good. From this poll we see that the needs people have are directly related to the central problem areas of life. What I am suggesting is that these needs can be fulfilled by centering action on a divine love. Personal purity, family morality, the caring, creative, loving community, and public commitment based on ethical ideals are all integrated through the comprehensive strategies of love. Full meaning from life comes as we purposefully and lovingly direct ourselves to each area of need.

Even a recluse like Emily Dickinson could realize:

> If I can stop one heart from breaking
> I shall not live in vain
> If I can ease one life the aching
> Or cool one pain,
> Or help one fainting robin
> Unto his nest again,
> I shall not live in vain.

We cannot run away from ourselves, from each other, or from the complicated situations with which life confronts us. We need to receive love and we need to give love in every relationship. If we can take responsibility with love for all relationships, then we make ourselves lovable, and thus we are worthy to receive love.

The Holy Spirit and Love

Once we enter into a covenant with love, we realize that there is a spirit that works for our well being at the other end of the covenant. We may call this God's Holy Spirit. Since God is a loving being, He seeks to bring all creation, especially human beings, to the fulfillment of His purpose. Before the fall of man, human beings were meant to mature in love so that they would reflect God's love. As humans are created in the image of God, we are meant to reflect naturally God's purposefulness and love. The task of maturing involves directing all relationships to an ideal of love. The fall of man from the Unification point of view occurred through the primary irresponsible action: the violation or misuse of love. Self-centered love, rather than God-centered love, became the object of man's desire and action. After this violation, from generation to generation, we see that human beings have mistrusted the covenant with God. We do not trust that God's love is the source and ground of our own being, nor do we feel responsible for exhibiting God's love in relationship.

We still want to experience an ideal of love, but as fallen people we do not want to take responsibility for creating that ideal. Dietrich Bonhoeffer, in his discussion of cheap grace and costly grace, makes a number of observations that bear upon this irresponsibility. Cheap grace, Bonhoeffer says, is the desire of man, the sinner, to be forgiven of sin without making much effort to cleanse himself of that sin. Costly grace, however, calls us to follow in the path of Jesus and thus overcome sin by perfect love.[2]

As with costly grace, devotion to the Holy Spirit is not something superficial; it demands total, constant consecration. If we are to enjoy the fruits of the Spirit, peace, joy and love (Galations 5), we need to cleanse ourselves of all impurities and reflect a pure love. "Do you know that you are the temple of God and that the Spirit of God dwells in you" (1 Corinthians 3:16). If we are the temples of God, then we must maintain ourselves in such a way that God can dwell with us. Since God represents the purest love, we must love purely so that God's spirit will find a home in us.

The Holy Spirit is a purposeful, directive force, as it seeks to enhance the value of all relationships. If we allow it to work within us, like an artist works with his material, then we become purposeful agents for God's love. Love, knowledge, dedication and discipline, however, are needed to allow the Holy Spirit to work effectively. "He who abides in love abides in God, and God in him" (1 John 4:16). As we allow the Holy Spirit to give purpose and integration to our lives, we begin to exhibit the wisdom, piety and virtue of the religious life. Such a life is originally intended by God to be the normal life, for human beings are meant to make all things holy through love.

Like the victor who, on taking possession of a kingdom, places in each city men to execute his orders and act as his regents governing the place he has conquered, so the Holy Spirit, the loving Conquistador of souls, places some divine gifts in each of the human faculties, that through His holy inspirations the whole man may receive His vivifying influence. Into the intelligence, the supreme faculty of the spirit from which radiates light and order over the whole human being, He pours the gifts of wisdom, of understanding, of counsel, and of knowledge; into the will, the gifts of piety; and into the inferior region of the sensible appetites, the gifts of fortitude and fear of God. By means of these gifts the Holy Spirit moves the whole man, becomes Director of the supernatural life, and more—becomes the very soul of our soul and life of our life.[3]

The Holy Spirit, then, is a great weapon in our strategies of love, if we are to overcome the obstacles to the realization of love. As we allow the Spirit to work through us, however, we realize that we must also struggle to maintain the effectiveness of the Spirit. Just as every prayer is neither offered nor felt with the same intensity, so too there are periods in our spiritual life where we feel unloving and unlovable; we may feel spiritually dry, empty, in despair. At such times we must still respond to the duty of loving, for love is a duty whether we feel the desire to love or not. God does not "request" that we love when we are in the mood. He demands love from us.

> The supreme happiness of heaven consists in submerging ourselves forever in the love of God; the supreme misfortune of hell consists in this, that the last spark of love departs from the heart. In hell no one loves....[4]

Being a minister who has read everything about the Holy Spirit and who can define its nuances with all dogmas and creeds does not guarantee that one embodies the Holy Spirit. Not long ago I attended a meeting with ministers that was arranged by the director of a Unification Church food distribution program. My desire was to see how our church could work with other churches in serving the needs of poor people. The meeting was held in a school building attached to the church of one local minister. As I entered the meeting room on the second floor, I observed about fifteen ministers sitting in school chairs. We introduced ourselves and I began to explain how we could work together in service to the community.

When I finished my presentation, one minister wanted me to explain the theology of our church. As a courtesy, I explained very briefly some basic concepts, then I renewed my proposal about food distribution. A second minister questioned me about my definition of the Holy Spirit, and as I began to explain a third minister interrupted by saying that my definition was definitely not orthodox Christianity. What followed was a bitter inquisition about true and false definitions of the Holy Spirit. If I were a heretic, then they could not work with our church. The meeting ended. I learned during this experience that no matter how accurate our definitions, the Holy Spirit was not to be found in that room.

The best examples of the Holy Spirit at work are the lives of Jesus and the saints, the sanctified ones dedicated to God's service. Since I am a lover of art, I often visit museums around the world in search of paintings that treat the subject of Jesus and the saints. Invariably these paintings reveal to me some new aspect of how the Holy Spirit works in the lives of those who dedicate themselves to God.

In paintings of the Annunciation Mary looks at the angel who brings her the news that the Lord is with her. Her posture is one of willingness to receive the Spirit of God and to commit her will and her body to serve His purpose. The white Lily that is often found in such pictures symbolizes the purity of Mary's faith, spirit and body. It is fitting, then, that Jesus should be born of one who is such a pure host to the Holy Spirit. When the three shepherds come to visit the Christ child in a field near Bethlehem, they are often depicted as simple, humble and innocent souls. Everything attending the birth of Jesus allows for the purity of the Holy Spirit to pervade the lives of all those who surround him.

Although there are relatively few paintings depicting Jesus' childhood, there are those like Giovanni Di Paolo's "The Child Jesus Disputing in the Temple." Jesus is in his Father's house engaged in his Father's business, and through study and discourse he prepares himself for the Holy Spirit to work through him with full power. When Jesus is baptized by John the Baptist, John hears a voice from Heaven, the Holy Spirit, saying, "This is my beloved Son, in whom I am well pleased."

After his baptism Jesus is led by the Holy Spirit to the wilderness for 40 days. He must now pray, meditate and consider the purpose of his mission. Jesus' course is the classical pattern that many Christians follow after they feel called by the Holy Spirit. After the period of purification Jesus is then confronted by the greatest obstacle to the spiritual life: Satan. As those who seek to serve God must overcome the temptations of the Devil, Jesus must show the example of triumph. When Satan asks him to turn the stones into bread, and thus use his powers—and the power of the Holy Spirit—for a selfish purpose, Jesus refuses. When Satan tempts him to jump off the temple, thus using God's power for show and spectacle, Jesus refuses. Finally, when Jesus is offered the power and glory of the world if he worships Satan, he refuses. Jesus chooses God's purposeful love over Satan's seductive power.

Numerous paintings over the centuries show Jesus teaching about the Kingdom, about love, about obedience to God, and about the life to come. Jesus' life is a complete manifestation of the Holy Spirit, for he constantly exhibits God's truth and love. When Jesus encounters sin, as in paintings of the woman taken in adultery, he does not close his heart to the sinner, rather he forgives her and instructs her to go and sin no more.

The Holy Spirit expresses itself through Jesus in many forms: through righteousness, humility and courage. Jesus drives money lenders out of the temple, he washes the feet of his disciples on the evening of the Last Supper, and he agonizes in the Garden of Gethsemene when he prays to God, in a last desperate hope that the people will respond to him, then looks to find his prayerful disciples, Peter, James and John, asleep beside him. Paintings that portray these subjects often contrast the brightness of Jesus, surrounded by the Holy Spirit, with the darkness around those of little or no spirit.

As Jesus is depicted being scourged, bearing the cross and being crucified, we see the contrast of love and hate. In Rembrandt's etchings of Jesus on the cross, a light suggesting the Holy Spirit of God is focused on Jesus, while the world is shrouded in darkness.

If we reflect about how Jesus maintains a stan-

155

STRATEGIES OF LOVE

dard of purity and love, we realize that he overcomes
great suffering to be the vehicle of the Holy Spirit. A
follower of Jesus, whom I would call a modern saint,
Dr. Martin Luther King, Jr., endures a similar vilifi-
cation and yet, like Jesus, his life is a triumph over
hate. The Holy Spirit most powerfully comes
through Dr. King as he speaks of forgiving his ene-
mies:

> Let us be practical and ask the question,
> *How do we love our enemies?*
> First, we must develop and maintain the
> capacity to forgive. He who is devoid of
> the power to forgive is devoid of the pow-
> er to love. It is impossible even to begin
> the act of loving one's enemies without
> the prior acceptance of the necessity, over
> and over again, of forgiving those who
> inflict evil and injury upon us.[5]

As Jesus was crucified and Dr. Martin Luther
King, Jr. was shot to death, the saints throughout history have been tortured and killed for their crimes.
What were those crimes? Faith, humility, steadfast-
ness, goodness and love: the crimes of the Holy Spirit. If the saints did not suffer at the hands of others,
they chose a life of humility and service to God and
the Holy Spirit. St. Francis preached the message of
brotherly love; St. Vincent de Paul dedicated himself
to the poor; St. Dominic trained preachers and educa-
tors.

156

While followers of God and the Holy Spirit have offered a redeeming love to the world, they have often been responded to with a vengeful hate. When I profess myself to be a "follower" of the Reverend Moon, I sometimes encounter a scornful hate by those who have not read one line of his teachings, and who themselves follow nothing but the vagaries of their own emotions. As Christ represents the greatest love, and thus the largest purpose, he also represents the supreme value. It is my own faith that Reverend Moon is called today to fulfill the purpose of establishing God's Kingdom of love on earth as it is in Heaven. He has dedicated his life to work to bring the human family together in love and in unity centered on God's love.

Members of the Unification Church in 137 countries represent every race, religion and cultural background. Reverend Moon's teaching seeks to renew the message of Christ while actively raising up human beings so that they fulfill the ideal of that message: one human family centered on God's love. Unity in the Unification Church means a unity centered on God's purpose, value and love. As I am a "follower" of Reverend Moon, I seek to unite with God, His principles and His representatives. I personally have not found any better representatives of God's love and truth than Reverend and Mrs. Moon. If I did find better representatives I would follow them, for ultimately I am seeking to do God's will, no one else's. The Unification Church seeks to be a model of a loving global family for the larger world.

I believe most people mistrust leaders of all types, especially religious leaders, because most leaders are not motivated by the highest purpose. The world has been led by people who have brought it to the brink of destruction. Who can be trusted? If someone comes along speaking about seeking to do Christ's will and establishing God's Kingdom of love, we immediately think, "How much is this going to cost me?"

It actually does cost a great deal to follow God, the Messiah, or any righteous teacher: we must give up our false and selfish purposes for a large and noble purpose. This is the hardest sacrifice in the world. Who is willing to really say, "God, your will be done, not mine. I will live for you, not for myself." To say this is to enter into a commitment that must be renewed each day, many times a day. In my experience, Reverend Moon is a teacher of righteousness, gratitude, humility, perseverance, courage, hope and love. Although the leaders of our church are imperfect people, as I am, and although our church is an imperfect vessel for God's love, I have not found a better community of faith and love. I believe that the church itself is like a school where I and others can learn to live the ideals of love. I may or may not like the style of my teachers or the shape of the school room, but I know I need education.

Ultimately, I believe God wants us to be "normal" people: happy and healthy human beings.

I know that is what I want for myself, it is what every person I have ever met wants, and it is the goal of our church. As I look at the world, however, I find most people self-willed, resenting correction, attracted to ephemeral and sensual pleasures, avoiding responsibility for the well-being of others, avoiding unpleasant situations and relationships, cultivating comfortable habits, and choosing short-term practical solutions to problems rather than long-term ethical solutions.

To become a "normal" person from God's point of view demands different character and action. God sets forth a value-system that is very demanding. God-centered normal people seek a universal purpose as the basis for their desire and action. They see the integration of all parts of life as a commitment to value. They seek to understand God's will and want to be corrected, however painful it may be, so that they can align themselves with God's will. They are willing to endure personal discomfort for the sake of comforting others. They are often impractical people in the eyes of the world because they think of long term solutions to problems and seem to ignore such practical problems as the need for a new suit of clothes.

James Fowler, in analyzing the stages of faith, explains the mature person of faith in the following terms:

State 6 is exceedingly rare. The persons

best described by it have generated faith compositions in which their felt sense of an ultimate environment is inclusive of all being. They have become incarnators and actualizers of the spirit of an inclusive and fulfilled human community.

They are 'contagious' in the sense that they create zones of liberation from the social, political, economic and ideological shackles we place and endure on human futurity. Living with felt participation in a power that unifies and transforms the world, Universalizers are often experienced as subversive of the structures (including religious structures) by which we sustain our individual and corporate survival, security and significance. Many persons in this stage die at the hands of those whom they hope to change....

When asked whom I consider to be representatives of this Stage 6 outlook I refer to Gandhi, to Martin Luther King, Jr., in the last years of his life and to Mother Teresa of Calcutta. I am also inclined to point to Dag Hammarskjold, Dietrich Bonhoeffer, Abraham Heschel and Thomas Merton.[6]

To change from a normal person in the eyes of the world to a normal person in God's eyes is to undergo the process of conversion. Literally, conversion is a "turning" from one reality to another. Jesus describes the object of Christian conversion when he describes the normality of the Kingdom in the Beatitudes (Matthew 5:1-12). The obstacles to conversion are numerous: the habits of the self and the ways of the world. The goal of our strategies of love, nevertheless, is to overcome all obstacles, within and without, so that we become Kingdom-builders of love, good, normal citizens of God's Kingdom of love.

FOOTNOTES

1 Dava Sobel, "Sex With Therapist Said to Harm Client", *The New York Times* (August 29, 1981), p. 9.

2 Bonhoeffer, pp. 47-48.

3 Luis M. Martinez, *The Sanctifier* (Boston: St. Paul Editions, 1982), p. 14.

[4] Martinez, p. 225.

[5] Martin Luther King, Jr., *Strength to Love* (Philadelphia: Fortress Press, 1981), p. 48.

[6] James W. Fowler, *Stages of Faith* (New York: Harper & Row, 1981), pp. 200-201.

Chapter 7

Conclusion: Images for the Future

When we speak of transforming ourselves and the world around us, we leave ourselves open for a great deal of criticism. For who has not talked about these grand ideals without being either a hypocrite, a demagogue or a dreamer. Every age has someone who espouses these ideals, every young person probably feels called to these ideals, yet the world remains filled with as much evil as ever. It is my belief, however, that every age must come forth with such ideals and every person must feel them strongly at some time because they are inherent in the human condition. We are meant not only to feel these ideals, to be moved by them, but to realize them, for that is our divine patrimony. Our cells are imprinted with a divine code, not merely RNA but GOD, and we need to unlock the secret of that code.

Perhaps the great hope of human history is that each generation rediscovers fundamental, ethical ideals, what Huxley called the perennial philosophy. It is true that almost simultaneous with the awareness of those ideals is the forgetting of them. It is as if each age receives the same truth (broad ethical ideals) and loses the awareness of how to realize that truth almost immediately. Jesus, for example, inspired many people by his words and his actions, but as soon as he was out of sight people forgot the meaning and the value of what he was doing.

Every age must hear the great ethical truths, they must always be given in new ways, sometimes from sources where we least expect them, and we must always struggle to embody these truths in our personal and collective lives. We must always overcome the obstacles within and without that would prevent us from realizing our ideals. We have discussed many strategies for overcoming these obstacles, yet perhaps the primary strategy is to focus on the ideals themselves. We need to have clear images of what we value, for without such a vision we perish.

The prophet Isaiah comes to a sinful people and gives them hope by reminding them of their original vision of a just God:

> Then justice shall dwell in the wilderness, and righteousness remain in the fruitfull field.
> And the work of righteousness shall be peace; and the effect of righteousness, quietness and assurance forever.
> And my people shall dwell in a peaceable habitation, and in sure dwellings, and in

quiet resting places.

Isaiah 32: 16-18

It is important for us to remember the visions of the past, for we find a continuity in the human struggle between the real and the ideal. As we look back we realize that we are not the first ones to struggle; further, we see the vision or the images we need to live by as forming a tradition, a legacy which is left to us. If we ignore the past we do so at our own peril, since there is never time for any generation to rediscover the value of human history through experience alone.

> Men act, in large measure, in the light of
> the futures they envision or project. But
> the raw material for their action comes
> from remembered ideas, words, events,
> images and models. Thus, their search
> for usable futures in any era will be
> grounded in their view of particular
> past.[1]

Americans are often called visionary or idealistic people, and indeed our history is rooted in grand ideals. When the pilgrims came to America aboard the Mayflower, they gathered together on the boat and formed a "compact". They pledged to God that they would renew the covenant with Him, establish a society centered on Christ's love. As Americans we need to remember the pledge that was made by these first settlers, for it is a worthy foundation for a na-

165

tion. Unfortunately, Americans broke their covenant as they killed Indians, violated the land and even
became intolerant of those who would worship God
in slightly different ways.

At the time of the American revolution ideal-
ism sprang forth in the cry for political liberty: life,
liberty and the pursuit of happiness, inalienable
rights, God-given to each of us. Coupled with the political revolution was a spiritual and moral component: the vision of American transcendentalism in
Thoreau, Emerson, Whitman and others that was to
blossom shortly after the revolution. Whitman, the
great spiritual optimist, could offer the vision of an
unbounded self and unlimited democratic vistas:

> I celebrate myself, and sing myself,
> And what I assume you shall assume,
> For every atom belonging to me as good
> belongs to you.
> I loaf and invite my soul....
> I harbor for good or bad, I permit
> to speak at every hazard,
> Nature without check for original energy.
>
> (from "Myself")

Whitman's vision is not only born as a child of
the romantic movement of the nineteenth century,
it comes alive in us today as we Americans feel the
power of "positive thinking", "possibility thinking",
and the unlimited potential of human nature. The
dark side of "Nature" which Whitman celebrates,

however, is also the American who enslaved black human beings and fought a civil war to purge the nation of its sins. Vision and violation of vision seem to be the cycle of American history. The vision inspires us while its violation destroys us.

Central to Whitman's vision is a celebration of material existence, and we find in his work the American's love of technology, whether it be a simple bridge or a boat moving through water (see "Crossing Brooklyn Ferry"). The twentieth century American has embraced the vision of technology, with its unlimited possibilities to serve humankind, in a worshipful way. Marshall McLuhan's ideas of a "global village" that would be brought about through modern media became almost sacred dogma in the 1960's. McLuhan believed that media such as radio and television, which could transcend national and cultural boundaries, would draw the world closer together as one human community.

Technology is certainly an important component if we are to have a vision of the future, but we must also see how technology has been misused. We need to look at the content, especially the moral content, of media to fully understand the impact on human culture. McLuhan's emphasis on the medium as the message distorts the analysis of the impact of the message. Does the television situation comedy "It's Your Move" really bring any community closer together:

167

In the early episodes of this new sitcom, the story line seems clear: This adolescent living with his mother and older sister makes his life work by scamming them, his friends, his teachers and, when he can, the guy living across the hall who's soft on the kid's mother.
The series concept is based on extortion, fraud, trickery and a lot of meanness in the fatherless family. [Jason] Bateman, playing 14-year-old Matthew Burton, earns more by his wits than his hard-working mother does as a legal secretary. And the helpless woman never catches on.[2]

The content of such a situation comedy will have real impact on human sensibility. We cannot arbitrarily believe that if this show is seen throughout the world it will necessarily draw the human community closer together. For more important than a particular medium itself is the worldview of a culture expressed by that medium.

Our worldview largely determines our quality of life. What we believe translates into what we do. The failure of a coherent belief system for many in contemporary western culture has led to the breakdown of personal and social values. This in turn has brought about individual despair and social anomie, personal isolation and the disintegration of community life. All facets of culture, from the dehumanizing structures of modern urban planning to the misuse of human labor in our economic system, reflect the breakdown.

Vision and public policy

If we understand our relationship with God and His original ideal of creation, we can bring transformation and restoration to every area of public life. We must, however, translate the often abstract images of our religious vision into concrete proposals for public policy. We can identify, for example, in writers like Lewis Mumford the standards of architecture that can teach us to live as civilized human beings. Certainly the dirt in cities like New York, the graffiti on subway cars, and the disrepair of buildings symbolizes a hate for human culture. Rather than the human culture of cities, we have the anti-culture of cities where we learn to become barbarians. The architecture of cities can promote spiritual values or impersonal forms of power. We must choose which images reflect the healthiest world.

The U.S. Catholic Bishops have done a great service to this nation, I believe, because they have addressed the question of economics from a religious, ethical perspective. Although I may disagree with a number of their conclusions, I believe they have asked the right questions about economic processes. How, they ask, does the God of creation and covenant enter into the life of human community, especially in the realm of economic relationships. "Every

169

perspective on economic life that is human, moral and Christian must be shaped by two questions: What does it do *for* people? What does it do *to* people? The poor have a special claim on our concern because they are particularly vulnerable and needy."[3]

Michael Novak, in his critical response to the Bishops' statement, could still emphasize that economic arrangements must respect the dignity of human persons and communities.[4] We might disagree about the nature of these economic arrangements, but we must perceive that God would primarily be concerned about the sacredness of human person and community. We need to bring God, and a worldview that follows from God's ideal for creation, into the nitty-gritty issues of public policy.

If God is not at the center of our public policy debates, the state will often step in to control and vitiate all areas of culture.

Totalitarian governments right and left have attempted to take over control of all functions of all institutional sectors of society: education becomes propaganda, industry is militarized, law is politicized, art becomes ideology, and so forth.[5]

A religious ideal should inspire us, in every area of culture, to standards of excellence, to commitment and dedication in service to others. Every area of public life is affected by how we live in relationship to God, to our vision of ultimate meaning and value. The covenant with God calls us to a life of civic virtue and an investment in social justice. Is this the ideal that motivates young people as they pursue "higher" education? "Alexander Astin, director of the Higher Education Research Institute at UCLA, finds in his annual surveys of some 250,000 college freshmen that young people are less concerned with altruism, with helping society, and more concerned with making money and getting power and status than they were in the past."[6]

A "higher" education, from God's point of view, would teach students to develop God's universal heart within themselves, a heart of compassion, care and love. Technical training, then, would come on the foundation of ethical, character training. Like urban planning and economics, the discipline of education is rooted in a worldview that goes beyond the discipline itself.

With the religious vision itself we must ask whether the structures that follow from that vision make for "corpse-cold" institutions (Emerson's phrase) or a dynamic life-giving, life-managing faith. Does the vision give us static images that pacify us as we look to the past, or does the vision give us images that allow us to manage the movement of reality. We need images of the future, although they need to be rooted in a sound knowledge of the past.

STRATEGIES OF LOVE

The Unification movement seeks to transform human culture by clarifying God's nature and purpose in relation to the human community. We recognize that there are now enormous divisions within the human family: divisions between east and west, north and south, rich and poor, mind and body. In almost every area of human culture there are grave antagonisms that threaten to bury us all. Could a loving God be pleased with what he perceives in the world? Could any loving human being not be grieved by such a world? It is our faith within the Unification movement that these ruptures and divisions must be healed through profound understanding, a clear vision, and a great love.

Reverend Moon is a man of moral vision and moral passion. In a world where most people are at best luke warm in their commitment to others, Reverend Moon desperately seeks to embody God's love for others. The media mistakes the man when they see the Unification movement involved in every area of culture and they believe Reverend Moon is seeking to enrich himself. If they looked at the content of these activities they would see the heart of an ethical love. Science conferences have been sponsored for the last fifteen years with themes such as "Unity of Science and Absolute Values"; ecumenical meetings have focused on "God: A Contemporary Discussion"; and even media people have been invited to discuss "Ethics and the Media."

I believe Thoreau was absolutely correct when

he said, "He who gives himself entirely to his fellow man appears to them useless and selfish." Certainly this is true as many people have viewed Reverend Moon. His concern has always been to comfort God by teaching individuals to live fruitful, creative lives and by helping families live morally while building joyful, loving communities: "...both God and love are the center of the universe. Then in order to become a universal man, where should you stand—on the outskirts or right in the center with God and His love. The center with God and His love is already there, and you are making yourselves acceptable to that center."[7]

Vision and leadership

The difficulty of believing in ideals and seeking to make them a reality is the difficulty of leadership. For to lead, as we envision the concept in the Unification movement, is to "draw out" the best of ourselves and the best of others: our divine nature and our divine love. Leadership is not limited to an elite group, for every human being is called to develop his or her divine nature. Everyone is called by God, and those who respond to the call, who desire to take responsibility, are chosen to fulfill the vision.

The leadership of Moses over the Jewish people came to him because he responded to God's call; he took upon himself the difficulty of leading 600,000 people through the wilderness. Moses led the people not to diminish them, but to teach them how valuable they were to God. He and the people needed to undergo much training. Moses was tested by God many times over a long period of time. Several times he had to give up the comfort of his family and his home. Habits are difficult to break, even more so for a slave people who do not know how to take responsibility of a free people. Moses leads with his knowledge and experience of God, his understanding of God's law and his personal courage. The Jewish people have only to gain if they receive these leadership qualities from Moses.

How does Jesus lead? Once again we have someone with a vision, a law, a knowledge of God and the qualities necessary to make the vision a reality. Jesus teaches people about the Kingdom of Heaven. He tells them that heaven is not in some far off place, but in the midst of them. He teaches them to pray that the Kingdom be realized on earth as it is in Heaven. Many people were of course delighted to see Jesus, to listen to his lovely words and to be healed by him. When, however, he challenged them to make the vision a reality in their lives, they reacted with hostility or just simply disbelieved.

Jesus embodied the greatest leadership quality: love. He was humble, gentle, and compassionate, yet strong in belief, in will and in action. He was ruthless only upon himself, for he would sacrifice anything—even his life—for the sake of God's Kingdom. Although Jesus wanted people to believe him, to trust him and to follow him, he never sought to diminish anyone in anyway. Rather, like a leader with a life-giving vision, he wanted everyone who came in contact with him to feel nourished and benefited. Jesus could be a living paradox by both leading and serving simultaneously.

People reacted to Jesus as they reacted to Moses, not because these leaders were diminishing them, rather because they were challenged to be much larger in heart and action. Many of us believe that if God sent a messiah to save the world today we would be comforted by his presence. On the contrary, the messiah would show us how we look in God's eyes, and we would probably be furious by his arrogant, idiotic understanding of us.

Suppose God sent as a messiah a black man from Africa, who then came to preach in New York. What would he have to do to get us to listen to him? Suppose the night he was speaking in a shabby church we had tickets to the Metropolitan opera. Would we go hear a black man whose name sounds foreign? Suppose some white people's college-age sons and daughters went to hear him and got inspired. Would we understand or want to understand what they were inspired about? Would we be thrilled that they became interested in this black man's teaching and works? If we eventually went to hear him, could we receive the message through the accent of the interpreter or the wild gestures of the speaker. Would we come with an attitude such as, "This man may say something that will challenge me to change my life?"

The best leadership in the secular world still involves a vision, an image of the future, that relies on the best wisdom of the past while propelling one toward the future. If one stays in a Hilton Hotel one can find Conrad Hilton's autobiography in every night table. Hilton explains that his success stems from the foundation his parents gave him. His mother, he says, taught him to pray and to work hard, while his father gave him a vision of success. A vision, a spiritual source of power and personal responsibility enabled him to be highly successful, even after many failures.

Peter Drucker, one of the foremost management theorists of our age, describes good and bad leadership in the following terms:

> Leadership is the lifting of a man's vision to higher sights, the raising of a man's performance to a higher standard, the building of a man's personality beyond its normal limitations....
>
> A man should never be appointed to a managerial position if his vision focuses on people's weaknesses rather than on their strengths. The man who always knows exactly what people cannot do, but never sees anything they can do, will undermine the spirit of his organization. Of

course, a manager should have a clear grasp of the limitations of his people, but he should see these as limitations on what they can do, and as challenges to them to do better.[8]

The quality of a man's vision, and the degree to which a man embodies that vision, will determine the quality of leadership. The core of the Unification vision is God's heart, an infinitely loving heart. We believe that God wants us to cultivate the human heart so that it resembles His heart. He wants us to develop a culture of heart, a culture of love, where the ethics of the heart prevail in every relationship and in every activity.

We believe God suffers from an ancient grief because of how human beings betray the sacredness of the heart. Last night I went to see a film about Mother Teresa. The love of this saintly woman, who has chosen to comfort the poorest of the poor, is a great reminder of how God wants us to love each other. Although I was inspired by the love she could joyfully offer to others, I could not help feel a great sadness at the scenes depicting the children of war. As wars rage throughout the world, we grieve for the innocent children who are torn asunder by the madness and bestiality of parents.

We do not yet live in a normal world and we never will, unless we turn from the habitual to the celestial. We need a revolution, a conversion of the heart, where we turn from all that we are doing and bow down in repentance before God. We are the heirs of a human and divine history. We need to give thanks to God and to the entire human race for the patrimony given to us. But we must also see that we are heirs to the sins of humanity. We inherit not only the good, but also the evil. We must be grateful for the gifts, and we must be repentful for those who have been plundered and destroyed.

For those of us in the Unification movement ideas are not just ideas. They offer us images that guide us along the crossroads of life and death. Although it is important for us to create within our religious communities the quality of life we want for the larger world, we are still more concerned about the larger world than our own communities. I am often asked why Reverend Moon spends millions of dollars on various social programs. I reply that he feels called to bring people together so that they can understand and love one another. We don't feel the need to spend a great deal of money on houses of worship; we do feel the need to serve others.

Many religious leaders get upset by the messianic claims made about Reverend Moon. He is trying to serve God by teaching people to love all nations, races, and cultures. He feels called by Jesus to fulfill the ideal of establishing God's Kingdom of love on earth. He teaches that God's will is to bring all religions into unity centered upon this ideal of love. Finally, he teaches that each of us should act like a messiah in fulfilling God's ideal of love in our family, our community, our nation and our world.

Who is threatened by this man? Only those who don't share the ideals by which he lives. Reverend Moon has only one hold on his followers: the quality of his thought and the goodness of his life. I would rather follow someone who had an American accent and who exhibited a higher standard of love, however I have not yet found such a person. I myself would like to have the strength and love to establish a peaceful, loving world without having to deal with any teachers. Unfortunately, I am not at that point. I need a teacher of God's love, and I believe the world needs such a teacher. Certainly the world needs many teachers. But let us look for what we most need to learn. We need images for the future so that we may have a future, and we need leaders to lead us into that future. We can overcome the obstacles within and without, and become agents of a redemptive love, if we effectively learn how to use strategies of love.

FOOTNOTES

[1] Martin E. Marty, *The Search for a Usable Future* (New York: Harper & Row, 1969), p. 11.

2 Gus Stevens, "Kid Con-artist supplants cute moppets of television past", *New York City Tribune* (October 26, 1984), p. 18.

3 "Catholic Social Teaching and the U.S. Economy", *Origins* (November 15, 1984, Vol 14; No. 22/23), p. 337.

4 Michael Novak, *Freedom With Justice* (New York: Harper & Row, 1984), p. 155.

5 Max L. Stackhouse, "An Ecumenist's Plea for a Public Theology," *This World* (Spring/Sumer 1984), p. 64.

6 Susanna McBee, "Morality", *U.S. News & World Report* (December 9, 1985), p. 55.

7 Reverend Sun Myung Moon, "Word and Deed" (New York: HSA-UWC Publications, January 30, 1977), p. 5.

8 Peter Drucker, *The Practice of Management* (New York: Harper & Row, 1954), p. 193.